The Profit Faucet™

The Foundation For Small Business Success

Ken Germann

Business Growth Strategist

Peak Profit Global
https://peakglobal.com/

Forward

I'm Charles Kirkland of Media Buyers Association. As a ClickBank elite affiliate specializing in mentoring agency owners on how to generate high-quality leads every month, I have been helping business owners like you grow their bottom lines with systems and automation and take their businesses to the next level, for more than 20 years.

I am honored at this opportunity to tell you about my friend and business associate, Ken Germann, owner of Peak Profit Global - a full service digital marketing agency and the author of *The Profit Faucet™: The Foundation for Small Business Success*. Now, I've known Ken for probably four or five years, and he is an absolutely amazing business coach. He's an amazing marketer, and most importantly, he's an amazing individual. Ken is the kind of guy that if you call him at 2 a.m. in the morning, and say: "Hey, dude, I want to bounce some ideas around. What do you think?" he would say, "Hey, Charles, that's going to work."

He's also the kind of person who will call you on your B.S. So, if you try hiding behind an excuse, saying, "Well, I can't do this because of some imaginary obstacle," Ken is the kind of guy who will call you on it. So, he's a straight shooter. He will tell you like it is. More importantly, he's the kind of guy you want to have on your side.

The Profit Faucet™ is Ken's step-by-step playbook on how to build the infrastructure and systems your business needs to achieve success and increase profitability with less work. It should be required reading for anyone starting a small business or struggling to get ahead. So many of these "How to" business books are fluff, intended to make you feel good without actually providing any practical advice. Ken lays it on the line. "This is what you need to do. Here are your business priorities in order and here are the instructions to show you how to do it."

If you compare creating your business to making a cake, most of the books I've found on business and marketing will show you a pretty picture of the finished product, but they list the ingredients in the wrong order and don't give you any tips on how to put the cake together.

From Chapter 1 right through to the end, Ken has laid out your winning business strategy, step-by-step, with a detailed outline of every task you need to tackle in order to succeed. This is not fluff. This isn't somebody writing because, "Ooh, I think it sounds good" or "People want to hear it's easy." This book tells you what you need to do to succeed.

Ken starts out talking about your mindset because, let's face it, most marketers and entrepreneurs don't have the right mindset to create a thriving self-sustaining business. Your mindset dictates how your business will evolve and Ken guides you to adjust your mindset so you have the energy and drive to make your business. Most marketers and entrepreneurs have the wrong mindset. If your mindset isn't correct, there's nothing you're going to be able to do to make anything else work. Mindset is critical.

Next, Ken jumps into your small business development, and this is the chapter I wish I'd read before I started my business - because if you start with the wrong entity or the wrong business type, or you don't have everything setup correctly, your new business will become a tax nightmare or an accounting nightmare before you ever get started. Ken will guide you through this phase, so the foundation of your business is solid.

Then he explains the value of creating goals and a vision statement, as well as setting milestones, so you can actually build on your success and see your progress, rather than jumping from product to product to product, never getting anywhere. He also explains brand identity. How do you create brand identity? What does your logo say about you? What does your business represent to your customers? Should you sell hard? Many people are just terrified to sell, or they feel they should always sell hard.

Ken will guide you through the selling process so you are comfortable, confident, and successful. Ken's B.E.E.P.™ process is brilliant and a simple way to explain the sales process. He also, explains everything all you need to manage each social media presence, and why you need to adjust your selling technique on each social media platform.

If you already think this is an amazing read, that's just the tip of the iceberg. This book is jam packed with winning strategies for the small business owner. If you dream of owning your own business, or you're struggling to break even, grab a copy. Read it. Lock yourself in a room. Take the phone off the hook. This is an amazing book, and is a fantastic investment for anyone who wants to start a business, or work in marketing or build their business online.

If I had read this book years sooner, I would have taken so many shortcuts, and grabbed so many valuable opportunities. Even now, I can see how *The Profit Faucet*™ will do wonders for the success of my business. Ken is an amazing entrepreneur, an inspiring mentor, and an incredible coach. I recommend you buy his book.

Charles Kirkland
Media Buyers Association
ClickBank Elite Affiliate

Table of Contents

Chapter 1 - Adjusting Your Mindset

If you are reading this book, you are about to embark on an exciting and unpredictable journey. You are about to launch your own small business, with the aim of following your passions to achieve financial independence. You've got a vision of how your life should be, and you've taken the first courageous step towards achieving your goal.

But, I bet there are a few people in your life who are warning you that you are on the verge of making a huge mistake. They'll tell you that a small business owner works around the clock, struggling to break even, let alone make a profit. They'll tell you that a small business owner can't compete against the big international companies, and that you'll struggle to comply with tax and salary requirements. They'll tell you to stick with your 9-5 job and your salary. They'll tell you that your small business dream is doomed to fail.

Well, I'm telling you that you can succeed. I'm not just telling you, I will SHOW you how to make your business thrive, so you can retain your passion and achieve financial freedom. We'll start by adjusting your mindset so you are no longer at the mercy of the people saying, "You can't succeed." This is your dream. It's your passion. It's your life. Together we can make it happen. You can be the change our children need to you to be. The future of our children lies in the hands of parents that have successful, highly profitable, and fulfilling businesses.

What is "mindset"?

Mindset is the single biggest obstacle that prevents us from achieving a life of prosperity, abundance, freedom, and wealth. By wealth, I mean spiritual, financial, and emotional wealth. So, how does our mindset affect our ability to achieve these things? Positive ideas attract positive results and responses, negative ideas attract negative results and negative response. So, a negative mindset can create the biggest obstacle to achieving all your dreams, simply because you are bogged down by the problems arising from general negativity.

In my experience, your mindset incorporates seven distinct elements of behavior and attitude – your approach to handling each and every one of these elements directly affects your mindset and your future success. In this chapter, we will discuss how you can adjust your ideas to align with a mindset which attracts prosperity, abundance, wealth, and freedom.

How do you change your mindset?

Naturally the first question to consider is: How can you change your mindset? Your mindset is more than an attitude – it is the essence of the most important story ever – your story. People don't buy your products and services, they buy your story. People buy YOU.

So, what do you want your story to be? What do you want your mindset to be? How can you change your perception of the relationships, situations, and events that affect your life, so you can achieve the results that you want for your life and your business?

When I work with clients, I use a tool called the <u>Energy Leadership Index Assessment</u> to take a snapshot of the client's mindset, as it operates on a daily basis and under stress. As an Energy Leadership Master Practitioner, I can use this assessment to create an action plan, helping the client adjust their mindset through a series of exercises.

In order to change your mindset, you must overcome **seven key challenges,** by changing your thinking pattern in relation to the seven elements of everyday life that influence your mindset. To explain how this is done, I will share pieces of my life story so I can demonstrate how I overcame each of the seven challenges that influence mindset.

Challenge 1: Work Ethic

The number one challenge to your mindset is your **work ethic**. It's fairly self-evident that your attitude toward hard work will affect your ultimate success and fulfillment. I developed my own personal work ethic at a young age, as I worked in my parents' family business from the age of seven. My parents had a landscaping nursery and when we weren't at school, we were working long hours to make extra income.

At the nursery, there were countless shrubs and trees in small buckets and large buckets and these plants would all get weeds in them. So, our job as kids was to remove all the weeds from the buckets. Our parents would pay us a penny a pot for the small buckets, and a nickel a pot for the larger ones. We became very efficient at it, so the next year, we told our parents we were raising our rates! We wanted a nickel for the small pots and a dime for the larger ones. Our parents agreed, and we continued getting more and more efficient, until our parents finally told us they couldn't afford to pay us by the pot anymore, so they set a salary for us, paying by the hour.

I worked in the family business from the age of seven until I was sixteen, so I learned every possible job related to that business. From the ages of seven until nine, I listened to everything my father said, learning everything I could from what he knew about landscaping, shrubs and plants, everything. And by learning all this, I was essentially learning about sales, because I was learning how to help people. Sales is about helping people solve problems.

In the landscaping business, sales are based on helping people make their yards beautiful, giving them all the necessary items they need to achieve their vision of a beautiful yard. At age 9, I was doing landscape sales, because if my father was busy when customers needed help, I would offer to help them.

My father and I have the same first name – we are both Ken – so when people would come into the lot looking for Ken, I would say "Well, he's going to be busy for about two or three hours, but I'm Ken too, so I can help you." They would laugh at me a bit, because how could a nine-year old help them with landscaping? I would say, "Well sir, I'm happy to help you for now, while you're waiting for my father to finish with the customer he's seeing now."

Twenty-five hundred dollars later, I had helped the customer. I would help him by drawing the landscape plans out with stones and dirt the same way my father always helped his customers. Once I drew up the landscape plans, we would place the plants in the lot so the customer could visually see how the plants would look in their yard. As I grew older, my plans became more sophisticated, drawn out to scale on graph paper and including all the design work. I reached the stage where I was capable of managing every job connected with running a landscape nursery.

We were similar to any farming family, where we all contributed because we were all dependent on the income from the business. This is how I developed my work ethic – we were voluntarily working 12 to 14 hour days in the summer, sun up to sundown, in order to help our clients so the business could make the extra money.

The problem with working in a family business, is that you are always technically the last one to get paid. So, at 17, I decided to move away from the family business into the restaurant industry. As you read through this book and learn more about my experience and background, you will see that I have over 41 years of history in the customer service industry, because every job I've ever done has been customer service oriented.

Challenge 2 - Setting Goals

You've probably heard of *The Secret* and the strategy of creating a vision board. The problem with *The Secret* is that a vision board is not enough. You can't simply set up a vision board and wait for the fairy dust to fall, so that all your visions magically become reality. You actually need to set a plan in action – there has to be work involved on your part in making that dream happen.

So how do you make it happen? You start by setting goals. The strategy I use – which I also recommend to my clients – is to start by setting a two-year plan. And you break that plan into 60-day cycles, and then you break that 60-day cycle into daily goals. They all add up to the overall goal, but the idea is to execute your business plan in 60-day cycles, focusing on day to day activities to achieve those goals. If you focus too far forward, you lose track of the day to day goals you are setting for your business.

This is about mindset, because you do need to focus on hard work and discipline to make this happen. There is no magic fairy dust that can help you build a successful business. You need to work, and work smart.

Challenge 3 - Set Boundaries
Boundaries help you maintain a sacred space or comfort zone so you are working with clients who have the same business ethics and standards. These boundaries ensure that you maintain your integrity and protect your reputation, while making your working day far more enjoyable and fulfilling.

In order to protect your sacred space, you need to be able to establish boundaries on your time and your relationships so you know when to say "No, I can't do this" or "No, I don't want to work with you." If you have worked in your own business, you know there are times when you encounter clients who have different ethical standards and expectations. You don't want to do that – you want to position yourself so you have clients who are a mirror reflection of yourself.

I believe the theory of the Law of Attraction – that we attract reflections of ourselves into our business. There is a lesson to be learned from each client who wants to do business with you. Don't be afraid to set healthy boundaries for yourself and tell people "No, I'm not comfortable with this." It is essential to protect your integrity and honor because your reputation is the only truly important thing in your life. It is the foundation of your business.

Challenge 4 - Problem Resolution
Your problem resolution techniques have a huge impact on your mindset. If you are trying to solve problems from either the Boss Mindset or the Victim Mindset, your problem resolution strategy will be to blame someone else rather than finding solutions to resolve an issue. However, when you use a Leadership Mindset, you are looking for a Win-Win situation where you can solve problems, and this approach has a far more positive and far-reaching effect on your business. Will you be a boss or a leader? Bosses tell people what to do, and they are not necessarily fun to work for. Leaders are people who lead by example – rather than delivering the message, the leader is the message.

My problem resolution skills developed through my computer skills. There's no other way to put this – I'm a geek. My first computer was an Apple 2 with 32 km Memory, when I was 12 years old. My parents joke that my first computer was actually a TRS83 but I don't talk about that much. I have pretty much lived and breathed computers for the last 36 years because my brain thinks like a computer.

Throughout my career, I've always been very good at top-down thinking and compartmentalizing problems into what is called root-cause analysis. This means I am looking at the problem from the top down, and I compartmentalize the issue by looking at different aspects of the problem and saying: "Right, this isn't broken – put this in a compartment and set that over here. This isn't broken… this isn't broken…"

Finally when I've eliminated every aspect that isn't contributing to the problem, I can focus on the problem compartment. Then we are free to focus on the central issue and ask: "How can we solve this problem to create a win-win situation so everybody confronted with this problem can find a solution?" This is the approach I am looking for when I work with my clients. It is what we call a Level 6 mindset, and it is something we will discuss more thoroughly later in the book.

Challenge 5 - Choosing Happiness
This goes back to life's choices. Whatever problem you are facing, the real challenge is your response. We can choose to be happy in our lives, simply through the way we look at problems and tackle life. I consider myself a happy person now, and I have learned the strategy for happiness through my experience. As a child, I was teased and bullied and this situation actually lasted well into my adulthood, right through my twenties and into my thirties.

With my first marriage, I married my best friend, yet I didn't realize at the time that I was incapable of truly loving her in return because I didn't have the confidence to love myself. Seven years into my marriage, we knew things weren't going well, so we started marriage counselling. After a year of marriage counselling, the counsellor said to me, "Ken, all this anger and pain you are carrying around with you can only hurt you and the people who truly care about the person you really are. As long as you carry these hot coals around with you, you will just keep hurting yourself. You won't find happiness in your life until you are prepared to let go of those coals."

Now I'm a very visual person, so I instantly saw an image of myself carrying these hot coals that could only hurt me and weigh me down. I could see the pain I was causing my wife and the pain I was causing myself, and I saw where the pain was coming from – and I realized that no matter how hard I tried, I would never get the approval I was craving from my parents. As long as I kept holding onto those coals, going back to the well, I would keep hoping that one day I would win their approval... hoping that one day I would receive that apology from them.

Within thirty seconds of seeing the visual of myself holding the coals, I dropped those coals and I felt a huge weight lifted from me. The next day, I went to work – I was working at Wells Fargo at the time – and during my lunch hour I visited an attorney's office in the same building and said "I want to get a divorce. My wife and I don't have any children. What do I need to do?"

I knew my wife would never ask for a divorce so it was up to me. My strategy was to pick a fight with her and when it came to the point of resolving the problem, I said: "I think we should get divorced." As soon as I had seen those coals, and visualized dropping them, I reached a turning point in my life where I resolved that nobody was ever going to steal happiness away from me. Happiness is a choice, and that day I chose happiness.

Challenge 6 - Self-Compassion

Happiness is a choice, although it helps to build a strong foundation of confidence so you can truly choose happiness rather than doubt, regret, or anger. So how do you build this foundation? Most experts advise you to build up your self-esteem, but in my opinion striving for self-esteem is a waste of time.

Self-esteem is based on having confidence in yourself and pride in your achievements – basically it can only grow when you are feeling good about yourself. You can't build self-esteem on a foundation of negativity – if you don't feel good about yourself to start with, how can you build a sense of pride and confidence in your abilities?

You actually need to build up your self-compassion. You want to treat yourself the way you treat a best friend who is in dire need of your help. One of the first elements of being self-compassionate is to realize that there are no mistakes and there are no failures. There are only situations in life where you do not achieve the expected results. So, you need to evaluate, apologize when necessary, adjust and move forward. Sometimes when we make decisions in our lives, we may hurt somebody unintentionally so it is important to apologize for that decision when you realize you've done something wrong.

This last step is probably the most difficult. About thirteen years after our marriage ended, I went back to my first wife and said: "I realize that there are two people in a marriage and not everybody is to blame for everything, but I take sole responsibility for our marriage not working out. I was not capable of loving myself, so I was not capable of loving you."

To me, self-compassion is about loving myself for who I am, accepting myself as I am, and trusting my decisions and choices, so I can be happy with myself. I don't need anybody else's assistance to be happy; I don't need anybody else's approval of my business strategies. My business is my dream, it is my passion, and it is my intention to serve and help others. When people ask: "Well, how much are you going to earn?" I explain that I measure my success by how many people I can help, and how many people can benefit from my business. Profit is the result of helping people.

Learn self-compassion – learn to nurture yourself as you would nurture your friends when they need help. Don't punish yourself for making bad decisions – there are no bad decisions, there are no mistakes. When you don't achieve the expected result, you evaluate, you learn, you adjust, apologize if necessary and then move forward.

The lessons are in the journey. There is no such thing as perfection – perfection is a form of procrastination. When you stop your journey to concentrate on making something perfect, you stop making progress. You're stuck in the same place trying to achieve some arbitrary ideal. The only way you can move forward is to continue to have the courage to keep trying and to keep moving. An important element of self-compassion is to have the courage to walk through the next open door and take the next step in your life's journey. Don't slam the door shut for the sake of staying in the one place.

Challenge 7 - Learning to Listen and Be a Leader
As I mentioned before, as a leader you do not deliver the message – you are the message. Listening is an important element of this concept, and this was not an easy one for me to master because I am not by nature a listener. I remember a funny incident when I was a kid that helped me learn the value of listening.

As a kid, I could never be wrong. We had a family cabin up in Minnesota, near Cross Lake and we had a lot of family living in the area including aunts and uncles on both my mother's side and my dad's side. When I was about 12 years old, we were travelling up to the cabin, and I saw a sign about the Continental Divide. Once you cross the Continental Divide, rivers don't flow south any more, they flow north. I swore that I saw the Continental Divide sign, but my Uncle Mike was insistent that we had not crossed it. We continued arguing as we drove towards the town, and we crossed a few rivers along the way. I was saying the rivers would be flowing north and Uncle Mike kept saying "No, we have not crossed the Continental Divide – it's not for another ten miles." He was getting annoyed with me for being so stubborn about it. As we were driving along the road, we saw a little bridge that crossed the Little Pine River.

"You see?" Uncle Mike said. "It's flowing south."

"No, it's not!" I argued. "It's flowing north!"

"I've had enough of this," said Uncle Mike. "We're going to stop at that bridge and I'm going to pull a compass out and I'm going to show you that the river's flowing south. And you're going to admit to me that you're wrong."

First, we stopped to do all our errands in the town, and Uncle Mike was on a mission to do all the errands twice as fast as usual, just so he could move on to the bridge and prove me wrong. And I was thinking: "Oh man, I am in so much trouble…"

After we finished the errands we climbed back into the truck and drove toward the bridge, and then we stopped. Uncle Mike told me to get out of the car and we walked toward the river. Uncle Mike took out his compass and he pointed at the compass and then to the river.

"You see?" he said. "It's flowing south."

I looked at the river and then turned to smile at Uncle Mike. "Doesn't look like it's flowing at all to me," I said and turned to go back to the truck.

I have carried that message with me all my life, because I understand that you can't always be right but you can always listen. When I went through 400 hours of training to become a professional coach with IPAC, the International Coaching Federation, one of the most important lessons was learning how to listen. From there, I also learned how to be a leader. Leaders listen. Rather than bossing people around, we lead by example. As an extension of this idea, we lead and love by example.

As I went through the 400 hours of training, I became a better listener. A quote from David Augsburger really resonates with me: "Being heard is so close to being loved that for the average person they are almost indistinguishable."

In Summary

The essential elements of a successful productive mindset are:

- Having a strong work ethic
- Setting goals for each activity
- Setting boundaries for yourself
- Having a good problem solving technique, looking for the win-win situation rather than finding people to blame
- Choosing happiness
- Developing self-compassion so you can treat yourself better
- Learning to listen and lead

Chapter 2 - Small Business Development

Are you unsure where to start when it comes to establishing your business? Here is a to-do list of all the key tasks you must complete to transform your business idea into a reality.

Naming Your Business

When you are ready to establish your own business, one of the earliest and most personal decisions you need to make is what to name the business. I recommend something catchy and memorable, a clever play on words to reflect the product or service you are providing. It can take time to come up with the right name, and this might involve some brainstorming with friends and family, consulting a thesaurus, and Googling your short-list of options to make sure nobody has already nabbed your brilliant business name. Many new business owners choose the most personal and seemingly easier option of giving their own name to the business. I'm not a fan of this idea for several reasons.

Your business will build its own identity and while you are personally invested in its rise to success, the business is also a long-term financial investment and it should stand as an asset in its own right. This creates a number of potential problems to linking your business name with your own name.

Think ahead to when you have built your business into a thriving and respected company, and you are ready to retire. You have the option of selling your business for a tidy profit to fund your retirement, but suddenly the proudly respected business name is a liability. The new business owner "Mike Smith" will not want to buy a business that built its reputation through the name "John Jones & Son." Yet if "Mike Smith" changes the name, he risks losing the brand awareness and credibility that made "John Jones & Son" such a strong market leader.

Swinging around to another scenario, imagine that a disgruntled customer goes to the media with a frivolous complaint, and this complaint attracts a great deal of negative publicity for your business. Any business is at risk of attracting negative publicity, simply because some people enjoy complaining loudly. If the complaint is serious enough to damage your public image permanently, you have the option of changing your business name and starting over. However, this is problematic when your name is the same as the business, as the cloud of bad publicity will be more difficult to shake.

Going back to our first scenario, imagine you have sold John Jones & Son to Mike Smith who is happy to retain the well-known business name along with its stellar reputation. While you are enjoying your well-earned retirement, Mike Smith runs your former business into the ground, leaving a trail of furious customers demanding restitution. You are no longer associated with the business; nor is anyone in your family. Yet you are all embroiled in the scandal, as the media and the general public will associate the business failure with your name.

If you do still want to use your name for your company, I recommend using just your surname as part of the business name, rather than using your full name. The surname on its own is not so closely identified with an individual so it will not affect the image of the business as deeply.

My first company was an internet service provider established in 1994, and called *Sky Point Communications*. I created the name based on the first episode of Star Trek Next Generation's, "Far Point." Eventually, when I was ready to sell the business, it sold easily because the name was an asset, linking the company to its own strong reputation without still being associated with me.

However, when I started my marketing and executive coaching agency, I initially decided on the name *Ken Germann Coaching and Consulting*. Admittedly, this was partly my own ego, and partly a way of honoring my father whose landscaping business was called *Ken Germann Nursery.* But as I worked through my business plan, I realized this name would not help me achieve my ultimate goals. I have followed my plan to structure the business to be operated like a franchise, so that when I am ready to sell, the new owners will have an easy transition into ownership and management of the company.

My exit strategy is to build the business up to a value of multiple 8 figures so I can sell it when I am ready to retire and travel the world, experiencing new cultures. I realized that the company would not achieve the desired value to potential new owners if I used my name as the business name. This would undermine the new owner's efforts to make a smooth transition as owners and managers.

My next choice for the business name was *Heartlight Partners,* which I felt reflected my personal sense of spirituality and my extensive 42-year experience in customer service. However, I found that whenever I told someone the business name, either over the phone or in person, they found it difficult to catch what I was saying. So, I figured the name was not catchy or memorable enough, if people found it difficult to hear the first time! I made the name easier to say and understand, by adjusting it to HLP Global, with the bonus of giving the name a sense of global reach.

However, my search for the right name wasn't over – I found that when people asked what HLP stood for, spiritually inclined people were drawn to the name *Heartlight Partners* but corporate people were not so impressed. I needed a name that attracted a corporate audience. I finally settled on *Peak Profit Global,* adding a spiritual tagline, *Changing World Economics One Heart at a Time,* to reflect the spiritual side of my enterprise. *Peak Profit Global* is easy to say, hear and remember, and it reflects corporate success on a global scale.

I am going to create 8 companies that will be owned by Peak Profit Global. I start each company as a DBA (doing business as) of Peak Profit Global. A DBA is a legal alias for your company. Once Peak Profit Global reaches $100,000 a month, I will remove this DBA from Peak Profit Global and spin Peak Profit Global off into its own LLC that is owned by Peak Profit Global. Peak Profit Global is a Sub S corporation. S Corporations can own up to 100% of an LLC. This is part of my asset protection and exit strategy. I'll talk about that in an upcoming book.

Each name I choose is all part of the Peak Profit brand and builds value for that brand and company. A healthy intellectual property portfolio that is trademarked or patented adds in the value of the brand and company. Those assets are unique to the company. They can be licensed or sold to other companies. With the branding and company naming strategy I am using it will be easier to sell the brands and companies for a good profit when it comes time to retire and travel the world with my family.

A unique catchy business name is a far more flexible option, creating a comfortable division between your business and your private life, so you can control the level of your public profile in association with its fortunes and your business becomes a valuable asset you can pass on when you are ready.

Structuring Your Business

When you are ready to start your small business, one of the first decisions you need to make is how you intend to structure the business. Will you be a sole proprietor, or will you set up the business as a corporation or a limited liability company? Your decision will affect how much tax you will need to pay, your level of personal liability, and it will also impact your access to money. So, you need to consider how you visualize the future of your business and what type of challenges you could realistically face, in order to determine which business structure is best for you.

Each structure has its advantages and limitations so you must choose the best option for your current situation and your long-term business plan. Ask your accountant or business attorney to recommend the best structure for your business, based on your vision and goals.

Sole Proprietorship

When you establish your business as a sole proprietorship, the business legally has no separate existence from you as the business owner. You can give your business a trade name, but this is simply an "alias" for your name and does not create a legal entity separate from you.

The main advantage of this business structure is its sheer simplicity and informality – you only need to register your business name according to local business requirements and you are ready to go! Your income and losses will be taxed on your personal income tax return just as they would be if you were employed by another company. This is financially beneficial, as individual tax. Even if you decide to use a business name, your invoices will be in your name, so clients will pay you directly. You do not need to open a bank account in the name of the business.

The primary disadvantage of this business structure is that you as an individual are directly liable for any debts or legal damages the business might incur. So, if you take out a bank loan, assuming an upcoming project will cover the debt, you will be liable for the debt if the project is cancelled. This situation can undermine your financial security for your personal life and the future of your company. Even worse, if someone wins a lawsuit against your business, you will need to pay the costs using your personal assets. Costs could be anything from a minor overdue debt to a potentially crippling financial burden.

The sole proprietorship structure places no limitation on the size of your business, so you can have unlimited employees. However, as you and the business are the same legal entity, you are responsible for undertaking the business role for each employee – withholding taxes on each employee, paying tax to the IRS and keeping accurate records of all your payroll activities. You must pay unemployment tax on any employees by filing a Schedule SE with form 1040 to calculate how much self-employment tax you owe. You can delegate these tasks to an accountant – depending on the number of employees, you could hire the accountant to work for you full-time, part-time, or on a casual basis.

You will need to check your state's requirements on worker's compensation, as this can vary state by state and according to how many employees you have. It is also a good idea to obtain business or general liability insurance for your company.

Accounting requirements for a sole proprietorship
While it is not mandatory, it is good practice to maintain separate records for business and personal assets so you can have a clear uncomplicated record of your company profits and losses. You can do this by using a separate bank account and accounting ledger for your business income and expenses, keeping hold of all your cash receipts and disbursements to track the outgoings.

Partnership
If your business will be owned and operated by more than one

individual, you could consider structuring the business as a partnership. You have two options within this structure – a general partnership or a limited partnership.

A general partnership works similarly to a sole proprietorship, except there is more than one individual managing the company and assuming responsibility for debts and other obligations. It is more expensive to establish a general partnership, as they require more legal and accounting services, and at the same time they are still at risk of unpredictable personal liability costs. A partnership agreement will outline the rights and responsibilities of each partner in relation to taking out loans and making binding business decisions.

A limited partnership is made up of two or more general partners plus limited partners who only serve as investors. The limited partners have no control over decision-making in relation to the company and they are not responsible for any debts or other liabilities. This requires a high level of complicated administration, so it is probably not worth setting up if you only have one or two potential investors.

Accounting requirements for a partnership
One of the top advantages of a partnership is that while the company has to file a tax return (Form 1065) reporting profits and losses, the company does not actually pay tax on its income; instead the profits and losses are passed through to the individual partners who report their own share of income and loss, on Schedule K-1 of Form 1065.

Corporation

Unlike sole proprietorships and partnerships, a corporation is legally recognized as an independent entity, separate from its owners. This structure is far more complex and expensive – one major element of difference is that a corporation can sell stock to raise funds. While this structure involves more complicated tax requirements and other regulations, it also has the significant advantage of providing the business owner with liability protection. You are not liable for the company debt, as the corporation can raise its own funds through the sale of stock, so your personal assets are not at risk from any claims against the company.

Cost is the main disadvantage of the corporate structure. Each state has their own set of regulations that a corporation must comply with, so you will need consistent legal assistance as well as accounting and tax preparation support to ensure you are following all the rules and regulations.

You will also incur additional costs through taxation. The corporation itself is subject to federal and state income tax, while shareholders are required to pay tax on their earnings in the form of dividends from stock, and you will have to pay tax on your own income. However, you can reduce the corporation's taxable business profits by paying a salary to yourself and other corporate shareholders. These payments are considered reasonable compensation so they can be deducted as a business expense and are therefore exempt from tax. Keep in mind that the IRS will be monitoring your salary to ensure it remains within the bounds of "reasonable compensation."

S Corporation

As I mentioned earlier, one of the key disadvantages of a partnership is that the personal assets of the business owners are vulnerable if anyone makes financial claims against the business. The key disadvantage of a corporation is double taxation, as the corporation is taxed, as well as the individual.

A Subchapter S (S Corporation) is a form of corporation that combines the financial benefits of incorporation with the taxation benefits of a partnership in return for meeting specific IRS requirements. For example, the business must be a domestic corporation, it is limited to a maximum of 100 shareholders, and must have only one class of stock. Eligible shareholders cannot include partnerships, corporations or non-resident aliens. Shareholders can be company employees, drawing a salary in addition to receiving corporate dividends or tax-free distributions. There are certain financial institutions such as insurance companies that cannot file as S corporations.

There are several significant tax advantages to filing under Subchapter S. The S corporation may pass business income, losses, deductions, and credits to shareholders, who report their income and losses on their personal tax returns. By paying distributions that are characterized as salary or dividends, the owner can reduce the liability for self-employment tax.

There are also ways for the S corporation to save money on corporate taxes, particularly when the business is new. The main drawback to these benefits is that the IRS will keep a close eye on all your transactions to ensure you are complying with tax requirements. Filing articles for incorporation is costly and time consuming, and involves a registration fee and annual report fees.

Limited Liability Company

Another corporate structure is the Limited Liability Company (LLC) which also combines the features of a sole proprietorship, a corporation, and a partnership. As the name suggests, members of a limited liability company cannot be held personally liable for a company's debts or liabilities, and it also has the same taxation benefits as a partnership. The LLC only files an informational tax return. It is not a suitable structure for a company intending to become publicly listed.

While the LLC combines the financial benefits of a corporation and a partnership, it is also a much more complicated structure than the other two. An LLC is easier to set up than a corporation but it must be dissolved if one partner dies or becomes bankrupt unless there is a business continuation agreement, whereas a corporation can exist indefinitely. The business continuation agreement sets out how interests should be transferred in the event of one partner's death.

An LLC Operating Agreement is also recommended as this document works as a binding set of rules for internal operations and compliance with state laws, while outlining the terms of the LLC as well as the rights and responsibilities of each owner. The Operating Agreement is not mandatory, but without it, you will need to defer to the default rules as set out in your state, and these rules might not resolve issues the way you wish.

Why You Need an Accountant

Whatever business structure you decide upon, you will be very wise to hire an accountant to handle taxes, payroll, and the general account keeping side of your business. They say there are two certainties in life – death and taxes. As a small business, you have one other certainty to contend with – the IRS is watching you closely, because small businesses are the biggest culprits when it comes to tax evasion. Even if you have no intention to cheat the IRS, it's actually easy to miss out on your tax requirements without an expert checking that you are fulfilling all your obligations.

One of the biggest taxation pitfalls for a small business is payroll tax. You can be liable for payroll tax penalties for failure to file, failure to deposit, or failure to pay. Once you file a 941 (Payroll Tax Return) you have 16 days to pay the penalties or you are hit with a crippling interest rate starting at 33%.

If you fail to file or pay your payroll taxes correctly, the IRS can refer your case to the Criminal Investigation Division to investigate whether your actions – or inactions – constitute a federal crime. If you accrue payroll tax debt, the IRS has the authority to put you out of business without obtaining a court order, so they can seize your assets and collect any upcoming customer payments to cover the debt. These costs can not only destroy your business, they can also decimate your personal assets, so you can see why it is absolutely in your best interest to ensure a qualified accountant is overseeing your payroll and your taxes efficiently.

The Benefits of Outsourcing Payroll

Payroll is such a precarious aspect of business management, so your best option is to outsource payroll to an external preparation service.

Time and Money

Payroll administration is a time-consuming task, involving bookkeeping, creating paychecks, and managing tax requirements. Even small businesses of less than 20 employees find it more cost-effective and efficient to outsource the task to a specialist in payroll services, who can streamline the service with a combination of expertise, best practices, and the latest software. A payroll specialist will actually complete the task faster and more accurately, saving you both time and money while providing your employees with a more reliable service. This means you and your employees are free to pursue other worthwhile projects directly related to the business, rather than being bogged down by administrative issues.

Compliance and Accountability

Payroll is notorious for its IRS rules and regulations and if you violate the IRS rules in relation to payroll, your business may be fined. According to figures published in BusinessWeek, forty percent of small businesses are fined by the IRS each year for improperly filing their payroll taxes. However, when you outsource payroll, you also transfer responsibility for legal compliance to your payroll company, who will generally offer a guarantee with their work. Professional payroll companies are not only more compliant and accountable, they also have more flexibility, as the IRS is generally more lenient about errors or late submissions when the paperwork is filed by a payroll company rather than directly by the business. If your company has employees dispersed in different areas, payroll services can help you comply with legal variations from state to state.

Managing Employees

The ideal employee is dedicated, loyal, and enthusiastic about coming to work each day. Full of innovative ideas along with the skills and experience to bring those ideas to life, this employee will be instrumental in helping your business grow and thrive.

But how do you find an employee like that? How do you ensure your entire work team is energetic and enthusiastic and loyal? Too many small business owners find themselves frustrated by apathetic employees who watch the clock all day and then quit without warning, just when they were mastering their responsibilities. This slows your business down, cuts into your profits as you need to start all over again with a new employee, and limits the potential to expand the business through the contributions of your team.

Full-time, Part-time, or Contractor?

For the small business owner, it is not always cost-effective to take on full-time or even part-time employees. In this case, you can outsource various tasks to freelancers. Personally, I prefer freelancers over employees for a number of reasons.

Firstly, it is simply more cost-effective to pay someone a fixed or hourly rate to complete a task, rather than establishing a salary or wage for someone who might not necessarily need to work a prescribed number of hours each day or week. When you choose to work with freelancers, you have the flexibility to hire people when you need them, so your payroll budget can extend further. This means you can hire a wider range of freelancers for various odd tasks – such as creating a complicated PowerPoint presentation or writing a series of blog posts.

Another major advantage to hiring freelancers is that your business can work around the clock. Through the Internet, I hire freelancers from all around the world, so they keep working while I am asleep. This means that my business is running 24/7, increasing productivity and profits by 300%.

Choose freelancers from reputable online freelancing sites such as Upwork. I prefer to only hire people with a proven track record of expertise and customer service, so I will only consider a freelancer who has clocked up 200 hours through the online site and has a professional portfolio and consistent positive feedback. Concentrate on quality rather than price and build relationships with your freelancers so you can create an online team of trusted workers.

As mentioned above, the ideal employee or freelancer is professional, enthusiastic, reliable and engaged with your business. If a freelancer proves to be a bad fit for your business, you can simply hire someone else the next time; it is not so simple to release your connection with an employee.

There are some simple strategies for building a supportive, energetic and cohesive team of freelancers and employees – all these strategies stem from your identity as an employer. To achieve the best results for your business, you need to commit yourself to being a supportive and inspiring employer.

Find the Right People for the Job

Your recruitment strategy is instrumental for long-term success. Your ideal employee will demonstrate a proven aptitude for the job at hand, through qualifications and/or experience in the field. During the job interview, the employee will talk about how they will handle the challenges and responsibilities, rather than how much they really, really need a job right now.

On your side of the table, you will offer a fair salary or wage based on market comparison. If possible, you might offer slightly more than the going rate – this gives you the freedom to choose from the best of the best; and your employees will not be distracted by better paying jobs while they are working for you.

Establish Clear Expectations

Once you hire someone, provide a clear and detailed outline of the job description so they know exactly what you expect of them. This also gives the employee the confidence of knowing what is *not* their responsibility, so they can stay focused on the job at hand without being distracted by irrelevant side issues, and they know who to ask if they have an issue relating to something outside their responsibilities.

In a small business, it can happen that employees will "help out" with certain jobs that aren't actually part of their job description. This means you are wasting your valuable resources on trivial tasks, when they could be working at something more suited to their skills. When every employee has a clear set of responsibilities, the team works more efficiently as a whole.

Set some clear goals and targets, so the employee knows what they are aiming to achieve, and can monitor their own progress and ability. This also ensures that they will communicate with you if the goals become unrealistic – for example, if the expansion of business means their workload increases significantly. It is more productive when your employees approach you about any workload issues rather than completing the job inefficiently.

Establish Strong Communication
Set up a workplace culture where employees are comfortable and confident about communicating with you, so your business can benefit from their expertise and their on-the-job observations. When you have all the latest information and feedback, you can keep steering your business in the right direction. Conversely, employees who are intimidated by the manager will keep pretending everything is fine, even if there is a problem.

You should also communicate clearly and regularly with your employees, so any issues can be resolved before they turn into major problems. It is a good idea to conduct regular performance reviews so you can discuss how your employees are meeting their responsibilities and how they could improve their performance. This should not be a blame exercise, but a way to offer practical solutions and support, such as additional training to master new skills or refresh old ones.

Encourage a Sense of Ownership
Your employees will feel more motivated and more appreciated if they are acknowledged for their achievements and their ideas. Encourage your employees to take part in decision making, as not only will they feel valued as part of the team, they will also be able to suggest improvements and innovations that might not necessarily have occurred to you. An employee who feels appreciated is more likely to stay loyal to the company and stay motivated to doing the best possible job.

Ask your employees for advice and opinions, and turn meetings into brainstorming sessions so everyone has a say. Each employee will have a unique and valid perspective on the challenges you face as a business, so you will gather valuable insight when you encourage employees to actively contribute to discussion and fostering change.

Maintain a Challenging and Exciting Environment
When your employees first start working for you, they are slightly out of their depth as their new role is challenging and they are uncertain about what the future holds. But eventually when they master their responsibilities, they have two options – settle into a rut and go stale, or take on new stimulating challenges.

In order to keep your employees with your company, you need to offer them the stimulation and variety they will eventually seek – otherwise they will concentrate their energy on pursuing another role with another company. Provide opportunities for advancement or additional training, so your employees keep their skills fresh and their enthusiasm high.

When you create a rewarding and nurturing environment for your employees, they will in turn contribute enthusiastically to your business.

Taking on the Global Market

Globalization is no longer confined to the larger corporation – thanks to the Internet, direct communication and faster mail delivery, any small business owner can expand into the global market. Taking on the global market is a huge challenge for any small business – not only do you need to contend with the logistics of communicating with customers all over the world and delivering goods internationally, you also have the challenge of adapting your business message to different cultural environments.

Unlike a larger more established business, a small business cannot gather the same level of financial support or conduct the same level of targeted market research in order to research new markets. However, a small business does have the benefit of being flexible and adaptable, especially if you start small and outsource where necessary to stay efficient.

Are you ready to expand?

A global market begins at home, so it is important that you have established your local market so it is running smoothly before you embark on your global marketing adventure. Your local market will help you maintain the revenue you need to fund expansion, and you will also have a better hands-on understanding of how to solve the problems you will face overseas.

Reassess Your Brand Integrity

We have previously talked about brand awareness and brand integrity. Before you embark on international markets, it is a good idea to revise your vision and mission statement and assess how you are keeping up with your original promises. Once you globalize, you need to be sure your brand message is strong and consistent and accurate, because if there are any weaknesses or inconsistencies, the brand message will not translate effectively into foreign markets.

If your message is not clear, the global markets will not understand your business and if your actions are not consistent with your vision and mission, then your failings will be pointed out on a global scale. When you are clear about your business' values and goals, you will be able to maintain your consistency when you deal with conflict in the global market.

For example, skincare company L'OCCITANE encountered a value conflict when they began exporting their products to China. L'OCCITANE has always positioned itself as an ethical brand that has strongly campaigned against animal testing. However, Chinese authorities require all imported skincare products must be tested on animals before they are sold to the public. So how does L'OCCITANE reconcile its stance against animal testing with the sale of its products in China?

In a statement on their website, the company says: "L'OCCITANE is fundamentally committed to the abolition of animal testing of beauty products worldwide. Unfortunately, given the limited economic and political weight of L'OCCITANE, ceasing to sell our products in China will not do anything to change local regulations. Instead, to move forward we decided to develop a relationship with the Chinese authorities to pledge the case for the ending of animal testing for beauty products, through open dialogue."

L'OCCITANE is one of the main beauty brands working with the British Union for the Abolition of Vivisection (BUAV) on a taskforce called *China Cosmetics Cooperative Group* dedicated to promote alternative testing methods for Chinese skincare products. This way, L'OCCITANE stays true to their values and their company mission and vision, despite the fact that some of their international markets do not share the same values.

Choose One International Sector at a Time

The world is not divided into US and "foreign markets." Each sector of the foreign market is unique with distinctive cultural and commercial requirements to which you must adapt your brand message. Research as much as you can, compare your business to competitors in the area, and study the local marketing requirements to ensure your product or service complies in every way. And just as you would put an office manager in charge of a new office in a fresh location, consider delegating a local manager for each new global location.

Work Out the Logistics

Simply attracting customers is not enough. You need to follow through by accepting payment and delivering the goods or services. This can be complicated from a logistical point of view, especially if you suddenly start attracting customers from different points of the globe.

Make sure your website can convert your prices to any currency, so your potential customers know exactly how much they are paying. If you are selling tangible products, you need to establish the resources to efficiently package and deliver any goods to customers within an agreed time frame.

Use Social Media as a Marketing Tool

Your social media platform is a powerful and streamlined way to reach out to your global audience of customers. Social media is both engaging and interactive, so a strong social media campaign can attract and retain potential customers. Of course, simplicity is the key to an effective global marketing message, to ensure your key brand promises translate effectively to global markets.

Outsource

You don't want to be bogged down by the endless administrative tasks involved in running your business – you want to be the passionate driving force! You can always outsource or delegate various tasks to other experts, in order to keep your business running smoothly and efficiently on all fronts. Delegation is a valuable investment as you can protect one of your most precious resources – your time – while still providing a professional and streamlined service to your customers. If you try to manage all these little tasks yourself, you will lose your passion for the biggest task of all – using your energy and creativity to always look ahead and see how you can best help the customer. We have several programs available to help you increase your sales, profitability, leadership skills, and productivity. If you would like to know more and get updates on coming events, please visit: http://peakprofitacademy.com.

Strategies for Small Business Leadership

As a business owner, your most important role is to provide leadership to your employees, your contractors, and your customers. As the business leader, you embody the spirit and drive of the business, and your example should inspire your employees to stay focused on helping the customer solve their problem through the use of your product or service. You are also responsible for structuring the business to ensure optimum communication and productivity.

Planning is an important aspect of your leadership, and there are four types of planning involved in managing a small business: strategic planning, tactical planning, operational planning and contingency planning.

Strategic planning involves defining your long-term strategy for your business, and then making decisions based on achieving the desired result. As the first step to creating a strategic plan, you must survey the business as a whole from the long-term perspective of the following three questions:

- What do we do?
- Who are we doing this for?
- How do we achieve the best results?

You can create a 3 to 5-year strategic plan based on your answers to these questions. Of course, the answers you give today may not achieve the desired result five years from now, due to unforeseen circumstances, known as "strategic risks." Strategic planning is generally undertaken by the business owner or upper management, as they have the long-term vision for the company.

Tactical planning is more immediate, involving short range planning (up to one year) in relation to the operational side of the business. These plans are the tactics you will apply to achieve your long-term strategy. As part of your tactical planning, you will define the role of each sector of the organization and what they are expected to achieve. Again, tactical planning cannot account for unforeseen circumstances which may create obstacles to achieving the desired result. These potential issues are called "tactical risks." Tactical planning is the responsibility of managers who are closer to a hands-on role in the company, as they understand the daily operational activities of the business.

Operational planning involves linking strategic goals and objectives to the tactical goals and objectives, in order to create measurable milestones, time frames for completion and to define the successful achievement of a goal.

Of course, unforeseen internal and external factors can derail the best operational plans, so it is important to "back up" your plans with a contingency plan to cover any unexpected event that could affect your company's profitability or professional image. Internal factors can include the unprofessional behavior of employees, a public relations crisis with a dissatisfied customer or a fire damaging company property. External factors could include a natural disaster or a market shift diminishing demand for your product. The tourism industry, for example, is particularly vulnerable to political upheaval or natural disasters that can suddenly turn a desirable tourist destination into a danger zone, leaving resort owners and souvenir merchants without a viable income during a difficult time.

Your contingency plan should include a crisis management plan, a business continuity plan, and asset security. The crisis management plan includes a SWOT analysis, defining strengths, weaknesses, opportunities, and threats, so you can identify potential challenges and create a strategy to handle them when they arise.

An important element of developing your contingency plan is to visualize scenarios that could realistically impact the security of your business, and then work out a plan to handle this scenario efficiently when it arises. For example, what if a senior team member took advantage of confidential access to customer information in order to embezzle money or as the first steps to establishing a rival company and luring away your loyal customers? How do you protect your intellectual property from internal threats while still giving your employees the necessary access to do their jobs?

The continuity plan involves identifying factors that could impact the continuity of the business, such as a financial crisis or the death of a key management team member. Comprehensive insurance coverage can generally guard against any financial crisis, and a strong delegation and communication strategy can ensure that the business can continue even if a key player is no longer involved.

Asset security refers to the security of intellectual property, internal computer network, key equipment and machinery and other valuable assets related to the operations and maintenance of the company. Basic precautions include a backup plan for computer records, a checks and balances system to monitor employees handling sensitive or confidential material, as well as legal strategies to counteract any damage from potential loss of assets.

In Summary

I recommend creating a unique catchy **business name** rather than using your own name for the business. A unique business name retains its brand value if you want to sell the business, and it also protects your personal reputation if the business goes through a difficult phase, attracting bad publicity.

When you are ready to start your small business, your first major decision is how to structure your business. Your options include being a sole proprietor or setting up the business as a corporation or a limited liability company. Each structure has its advantages and limitations, in relation to your level of personal liability, taxation, and your access to funding from banks.

When you establish a **sole proprietorship,** the business legally has no separate existence from you as business owner. The advantage of this structure is its informal simplicity; the disadvantage is your lack of personal protection if the business incurs debts. It is good practice to maintain separate records for your business and personal assets.

There are two types of **partnerships – general and limited.** A general partnership is similar to a sole proprietorship except there is more than one individual managing the company and assuming responsibility for debts and other obligations. A partnership agreement can outline the rights and responsibilities of each partner. A limited partnership also includes limited partners who only serve as investors and have no control over decision making.

A **corporation** is legally recognized as an independent entity, separate from its owners. This provides owners with liability protection, although it does involve more complicated tax requirements and other regulations. An **S Corporation or Subchapter S** combines the financial benefits of incorporation with the tax benefits of a partnership in return for meeting specific IRS requirements.

A Limited Liability Company (LLC) combines the features of a sole proprietorship, a corporation, and a partnership. Members of a limited liability company cannot be held personally responsible for a company's debts or liabilities and it has the same taxation benefits as a partnership. It is not a suitable structure for a company intended to be publicly listed.

Regardless of which structure you choose, you should hire an accountant to manage payroll and taxes, as one of the biggest taxation pitfalls for small business is payroll tax. If you fail to file, deposit, or pay your tax, the IRS has the authority to put you out of business without obtaining a court order. They can seize your assets and collect any upcoming customer payments to cover the debt.

Your **ideal employee** is dedicated, loyal, and enthusiastic, with the skills and experience to match. Your management style will directly impact the enthusiasm and loyalty of your team, and there are strategies you can utilize to encourage your team to give their best at all times.

From a financial perspective and a business perspective, **freelancers** can be a better option than employees. Hiring freelancers gives you greater flexibility as you have specialized expertise at your fingertips, you only need to pay people when you need them, plus you can establish a global team, keeping your business running 24 hours a day, increasing your productivity and profit by 300%.

Thanks to the Internet, direct communication and airmail, globalization is now a realistic option for a small business. However, it is a logistical challenge as you need to establish efficient and consistent delivery and communication, while adapting your business message to different cultural environments. While you cannot command the same level of financial support as larger international companies, you have the advantage of flexibility as you start small and outsource when necessary.

Start by **establishing your local market** so it is running smoothly. As you take on foreign markets, you will need to **reassess your brand message** to ensure it remains clear, strong and consistent in a different cultural environment. Choose **one foreign sector at a time**, so you can concentrate on finding your niche and ensuring your product or service complies with their conditions. A **local manager** for each global location can bridge any cultural gap and handle any local business issue directly.

As part of your **leadership role**, you are responsible for structuring the business to ensure optimum communication and productivity. **Strategic planning** involves defining your long-term business strategy and making the necessary decisions to achieve the required result. **Tactical planning** involves immediate short range planning, creating the tactics required to achieve your long-term strategy. **Operational planning** involves linking strategic goals and objectives to the tactical goals and objectives in order to create measurable milestones, timeframes and to define the successful achievement of each goal.

Contingency plans work as a back-up, to cover any unexpected internal or external factors that could impact upon your company's profitability or professional image. Internal factors include unprofessional employees, a public relations crisis or damage to essential equipment. External factors could include a market shift or a natural disaster. Craft your contingency plan by visualizing realistic scenarios that could impact your business security. Your contingency plan should include a **crisis management plan**, a **business continuity plan,** and **asset security**.

The crisis management plan includes a SWOT analysis to identify potential challenges and possible strategies. The continuity plan identifies factors that could impact the continuity of the business and identifies strategies such as insurance to protect the business. Asset security involves protecting the security of intellectual property and the internal computer network, as well as equipment and machinery.

Chapter 3: Creating Your Vision and Mission Statements

Whether you are planning to start a business or you want to refine and strengthen your current business, you are guided by a vision that you have created in your mind. You have created this vision because you can see something lacking in your community, and you have recognized that you have the skills and expertise to fulfil that need.

The first challenge on the road to success is to shape your fairly intangible abstract vision into a series of concrete statements, explaining to the world exactly what you want to achieve and how you intend to achieve it. You need to make these statements both inspiring and succinct, so that others understand your goal and like-minded people will be attracted to the challenge of helping you make this vision a reality. When you articulate your vision, you will find it easier to break it down into smaller goals and stay focused on exactly what you want to achieve.

What is a vision statement?

A vision statement is the statement that articulates your vision, clearly communicating exactly what you are striving to achieve. Your vision statement describes your perfect community exactly as you wish it to be.

Look at the vision statement of Amnesty International:
Our vision is of a world in which every person – regardless of race, religion, ethnicity, sexual orientation or gender identity – enjoys all

of the human rights enshrined in the Universal Declaration of Human Rights (UDHR) and other internationally recognized human rights standards. The UDHR states that the "the recognition of the inherent dignity and of the equal and inalienable rights" of all people is "the foundation of freedom, justice and peace in the world."

For a more corporate example of an excellent vision statement, let's look at Apple's current vision statement, created by CEO Tim Cook:

We believe that we are on the face of the earth to make great products and that's not changing. We are constantly focusing on innovating. We believe in the simple not the complex. We believe that we need to own and control the primary technologies behind the products that we make, and participate only in markets where we can make a significant contribution. We believe in saying no to thousands of projects, so that we can really focus on the few that are truly important and meaningful to us. We believe in deep collaboration and cross-pollination of our groups, which allow us to innovate in a way that others cannot. And frankly, we don't settle for anything less than excellence in every group in the company, and we have the self-honesty to admit when we're wrong and the courage to change. And I think regardless of who is in what job those values are so embedded in this company that Apple will do extremely well.

Both these vision statements are extremely long, but a good vision statement can also be a short sentence or phrase. For example, the vision statement for Meals on Wheels is simply: *Well-nourished and independent communities.*

In each of these vision statements, you can see the writer has described an ideal community where the problems they see now no longer exist. The two longer statements are easy to read and all three are easy to understand. They are also inspiring: we all want to live in a community where every person enjoys human rights, where we settle for nothing less than excellence, and where everybody is well-nourished and independent.

Summarizing what your vision statement should be:
- Your ideal vision for your community
- Written with an inspiring tone so others are drawn to help you achieve your vision
- Easy to read aloud and easy to understand
- A comprehensive view to include a wide range of perspectives

Your vision statement does not explain *how* you intend to achieve this goal of a perfect community – that is the task of the mission statement.

What is a mission statement?

A mission statement is an action-oriented variation of the vision statement. While the vision statement described the perfect community, the mission statement refers to the problem that must be solved in order to create that perfect community. The Meals on Wheels mission statement says:

Meals on Wheels SA provides support to members of the community to live independently.

Our support enhances lifestyles through:
- *the delivery of nourishing meals to maintain health and well-being;*
- *offering social contact; and*
- *recognizing, responding and building people's capacity to meet nutritional and other needs that increase wellbeing.*

61

In providing these services through our volunteer workforce we strengthen communities. This activity is expressed as 'more than just a meal'.

So, you can see that when Meals on Wheels created their vision statement "Well-nourished and independent communities" they had a specific plan of action to achieve that vision. They intend to deliver meals and provide social support to people who would otherwise be lonely, isolated, and unable to fend for themselves. Even though it's not specifically mentioned in the vision statement or the mission statement, the provision of this service helps elderly and disabled people to remain living independently in their own homes rather than going into care accommodation.

Summarizing what your mission statement should be:
- Succinct, using short sentences that are straight to the point
- Action oriented, explaining what you are going to do to achieve your vision
- Broad statements

Why You Need Vision and Mission Statements
Your vision and mission statements help your organization identify the central issue you are striving to resolve and outline your strategies to achieve your vision. The most important purpose of the vision and mission statements is to keep your team focused. It is easy to get side tracked by secondary issues or bogged down by administrative details – if you get off track, your vision and mission statements help you take a deep breath and remind yourself what you are working to achieve.

Your team is stronger and more efficient when you are working together with a clear shared vision and a strong plan of action. The other essential purpose of the vision and mission statement is to help you build a network beyond your own team. When you provide a public snapshot of your vision to others outside your team, they immediately understand what you are doing and how you intend to do it.

This clear image gives your organization more credibility, and it shows other organizations and individuals how they can contribute or support your vision, particularly if they have visions that correspond or overlap with yours. This support will strengthen your organization and help you achieve your goals more efficiently.

In summary, vision and mission statements serve the purpose of:

- Keeping your organization focused on your shared vision as you create strategies to achieve your goal
- Inspiring others to support and contribute to achieving your vision
- Creating a central point to work from, while designing a plan of action and long-term strategies.
- Demonstrating exactly how you intend to achieve your goals
- Presenting a professional and focused image to outside sources, thereby encouraging potential customers and investors to support your vision

My Vision/Mission

My vision is to help my clients achieve freedom in all three key sectors of their lives – lifestyle, family, and finances. I developed the Profit Faucet™ so that I could help my clients develop the skills and strategies they need to achieve that freedom in their lifestyle, family and finances.

My mission is to give my clients the tools to make decisions based on "Should I..." rather than "Can I...?" When you are limited by time constraints or financial constraints, you need to ask yourself "Can I..." before you make any decision. "Can I afford this?" or "Can I manage this on top of my other responsibilities?" So, you don't always make the right decision for your quality of life or the best decision to enrich your future – you make the decision that fits best within the constraints imposed upon you.

When you free yourself from these constraints, you have the freedom to make decisions based upon your personal perspective. Rather than saying "Can I afford to send my kids to private school?" you can ask yourself "Should I send the kids to private school or public school?" Sometimes the more expensive choice seems more desirable simply because it is unattainable, in the same way it is difficult to concentrate on work if you don't have enough quality leisure time. When you have the freedom to make your decisions without being influenced by financial or time constraints, you will make better choices for yourself.

Creating Your Vision and Mission Statements

Of course, it is easy to create a vision of an ideal world within your mind, and just as easy to think up straightforward solutions to the problems you see all around you. It is another thing to encapsulate your vision into a short inspiring series of sentences, and then follow that with a mission statement outlining a clear and practical plan of action. So how do you begin?

Consult With Your Community

An effective and balanced vision statement reflects the views and vision of the entire community, not just one individual. As an individual, your view is limited to your experience and perspective so you can gain valuable insight by brainstorming your vision with other members of the community, to ensure the vision statement reflects the vision of the broader community.

So, the first step in crafting your vision statement is to define the community vision by gathering information and viewpoints from different members of the community.

Following are the questions you need to ask when you are consulting with members of the community:

- What is your vision for our community?
- In your view, what are the current strengths and weaknesses of our community?
- What do you think we need to change?
- What do you see as the major issues facing our community? What are your individual concerns?
- What are your expectations of our organization? What do you hope we will achieve?

There are a few strategies for gathering this information:
- Conduct a public forum so that community members

can brainstorm their ideas, observations, and opinions about their vision for the community. This forum can focus on identifying the current strengths and weaknesses of the community and discuss what type of changes and developments the community wants to see. You can keep a written record of the forum discussion to assist with future refining and planning.

- Hold focus groups for specific community groups, so they can express their unique perspective of the strengths and weaknesses of the community and their vision for how your organization can bring about positive change.

Identify Your Focus

You cannot solve every problem in the world but you can focus on one key issue in your community and strive to fill that specific need. Your vision and mission statements must be written around that central need.

You also need to factor in the type of organization you are running – for example, you may be a corporate organization with an ethical vision, or a non-profit organization striving to improve conditions for one sector of the community or a charity organization. Your vision and mission statements need to reflect the structure of your organization so that your team and the wider community understand exactly what you represent and what you pledge to achieve.

Brainstorm the Wording

Finally, you have reached the point where you can look at all your notes and confer with your team about the best way to express your vision so it is comprehensive, inspiring, and true to your goals. Try putting the key points in note form and then expanding them into sentences, to create a holistic vision statement.

Once you have written your vision statement, you can move on to your mission statement. This is a concise action-based statement giving a general overview of what you plan to do to achieve your vision and how you intend to accomplish your goals.

It is very important to keep revising your vision and mission statements until everyone in the team is confident that the statements reflect the vision and the mission of your organization. You should all be united in your commitment to achieve these goals, and this begins by agreeing on the exact wording of the key message.

Promote Your Vision and Mission Statements
Now your message is ready to share with the world! The next step is to work out how and where you will be promoting your vision and mission statements. Place them prominently on your website so they act as a snapshot of your organization's vision and mission. This way, anyone viewing your website will see an instant summary of your organization's goals and strategies. You can also include the statements in any press releases or media statements, and if they are short enough, you can add them to your letterhead or stationery.

In Summary
Your vision and mission statements provide a consistent and

coherent summary of your goals and your plan of action. These statements are the central pillar of your organization, ensuring you can stay focused on the job at hand as individuals and as a united team, and helping you build a strong productive network of supporters beyond your organization. Your vision and mission statements create the foundation of your brand identity which we will discuss in the next chapter.

Chapter 4 – Establish Your Brand Identity

A brand is a distinct name, symbol, term, or design that identifies your product, goods or services so they are instantly recognizable and associated with value and reliability – also known as brand equity.

As a small business owner, you may assume that branding is a luxury reserved for the big companies. Many small business owners make this call, deciding to channel their funds into other aspects of the business rather than investing in a unique brand identity and building brand equity. Without that unique identity, you merge your identity with all the other branded small businesses in your field – you are "one of the competition," indistinguishable from all the other unbranded businesses. A unique brand identity in the marketplace is the difference between being stuck at earning only 1% of your company's potential revenue to having the ability to double or triple your sales within a year – you might even increase your sales five times over with a strong brand identity.

What is a brand?

So why is your brand important to your business? How can a unique brand identity make such a difference in sales? Imagine if every business in your field was a square on a checkerboard – the branded businesses each have their own vivid distinctive color, while the unbranded businesses are the same shade of grey. Now imagine a customer comes along to select a color on the checkerboard. Naturally, the customer will ignore the huge shaded area where all the businesses merge together, and will choose a vivid color that appears to reflect their business needs. Which section of the checkerboard do you want to represent your business?

When your business looks identical to all your competitors, the only variable you can introduce is price. So rather than being completely indistinguishable on the grey section of the checkerboard, you have a little marker to indicate "cheapest service."

Apart from minimizing your profits, there are a few downsides to this business strategy. First of all, you are attracting customers who value a bargain over quality, so you are striving to finish the job in record time with a focus on cutting costs rather than delivering your best work. Your customers are not treating you with respect for your expertise, and you will be taking work because you have to, rather than choosing projects that attract you. Secondly, when another "grey" company tries the same cost-cutting strategy, you will be forced to lower your fees even further if you want to remain distinctive in the grey patch.

When even your customers can't distinguish you from the competition, they can't build a sense of trust and loyalty in your brand, so they will transfer to the next cheapest option. You have set yourself on a downward spiral, where you are scrambling for work without making sufficient profit; at the same time, you are losing your passion for your work by compromising with clients who do not value a quality result.

So, how do you start the process of differentiating yourself from the competition?

Building Brand Equity

Brand equity is the tangible value of your brand. There are several key elements to a strong foundation of brand equity. Your brand itself is one element – this should be a unique recognizable name, term, symbol, or design that identifies your business, differentiating you from the competition. As this symbol or term becomes instantly recognizable to more and more people, its market value or brand equity increases. This is an important long term strategy for building recognition and loyalty so you can create a steady growing customer base.

Your brand message is another essential element of your brand. This is your opportunity to explain the features and benefits of your product, as well as the values behind your brand, so your customers understand why they should choose your product over the competition. For example, today's customers are extremely conscious of environmental issues so many people will choose a brand with an environmentally friendly brand message. Keep in mind that your brand message must be a genuine reflection of your company values and practices. If you promote yourself as supporting certain values, you must live up to your message or your brand will lose credibility.

In order to create a consistent, genuine, and marketable brand message, you will need to research what your target customer wants from your brand, and how your competition have presented their own unique products and services. From here, you can build a brand strategy, working out how you will and will not promote your product, so your brand message accurately reflects your practices and appeals to your target customer.

Logos and Slogans

Some of your target customers will be visual so they will respond strongly to a simple, artistic symbol that reflects your brand message. For these customers, you need a colorful eye-catching logo. Other target customers have more of a verbal response, so you need a catchy slogan – also known as a tagline – which is a succinct memorable phrase that summarizes your brand message. When the slogan and the logo are combined, they become a powerful marketing tool, enabling the general public to instantly think of you in relation to your key product or service.

The Key to the Right Slogan

The right slogan can have a huge impact on the market, by directly influencing how people consider the product while the best slogans actually become part of everyday language. For example, De Beer's 1948 deceptively simple slogan, "A diamond is forever" launched the engagement ring industry by changing the average buyer's perception of diamonds – a diamond wasn't simply some impossibly expensive and unnecessary luxury. It was now the symbol of eternal romance and worth every cent because of course, the diamond and the romance would both last forever.

Other iconic slogans include:
- *All the news that's fit to print* - The New York Times, 1896
- *Good to the last drop* – Maxwell House Coffee, 1915
- *Say it with flowers* – FTD (Interflora) 1917

- *Snap! Crackle! Pop!* – Kellogg's Rice Krispies, 1932
- *When you care enough to send the very best* – Hallmark, 1934
- *The milk chocolate melts in your mouth, not in your hand* – M&Ms, 1954
- *Beanz means Heinz* – Heinz Baked Beans, 1967
- *Because I'm worth it* – L'Oreal, 1973
- *Capitalist tool* – Forbes, 1979
- *When it absolutely, positively has to be there overnight* – Federal Express, 1982
- *Just do it* – Nike, 1987
- *Maybe she's born with it. Maybe it's Maybelline* – Maybelline cosmetics, 1991

So, what are the elements of a timeless slogan? Firstly, you need to highlight the central benefit of your product from the perspective of your client. For example, *"Say it with flowers"* responds to the need of anyone who is wondering how to say, "I'm sorry/ I love you/ thank you/deepest condolences." The two cosmetic companies Maybelline and L'Oreal have taken slightly different approaches – Maybelline's *Maybe she's born with it* is telling women they can look naturally beautiful, while L'Oreal is empowering women to indulge themselves with the slogan *Because I'm worth it.*

The slogan should also differentiate itself from the competition. You can never be completely different from your competitors, but you can be better. Your slogan can demonstrate your dedication and commitment to doing better than everyone else. Other chocolate bars melt in your hand but M&Ms will melt in your mouth; other courier companies will deliver your parcel, but Federal Express will "absolutely, positively" get it there overnight. You might only be sending a card to a friend or loved one, but you can show you "care enough" by sending a Hallmark card.

However, while you are highlighting benefits and differentiating from competitors, avoid any direct comparisons. Maxwell House can live up to the slogan *"Good to the last drop"* but you can undermine your credibility with a slogan stating that you are the Number 1 or the Most Popular. Concentrate on honestly stating your own proven strengths and unique benefits, so you can live up to your promises without encouraging customers to make direct comparisons with your competitors.

Finally, a good slogan is short with a natural rhythm – the longer it is, the more rhythm it should contain. A rule of thumb is that slogans should be no longer than eight words, although longer slogans can work if they have a natural rhythmic quality to keep them memorable.

Avoid Jargon
When you are working out a catchy relevant phrase for your business, it can be tempting to fall back on the latest jargon or buzzwords. However, this strategy can undermine the strength of your slogan.

A slogan is intended to be simple, memorable, and straightforward, yet jargon is intended to obscure the real meaning and make the speaker sound more important and officious. A jargon-free slogan should be clear and to the point with no obscure references and no false promises.

Well known jargon terms, such as "in the field" or "cutting edge" have become meaningless through over-use... in fact, someone decided to improve on "cutting edge" by saying "bleeding edge." It is easy to misunderstand a jargon term - such as "in the swim lane" meaning sticking to your role – but worst of all, jargon can have a secondary tasteless meaning. For example, "drinking the Kool Aid" means following your leader's orders, no matter what, and it refers to a tragedy when a religious cult leader convinced his followers to drink poisoned Kool Aid.

Advertising jargon is notorious for being misleading so you can undermine your credibility by underestimating your target customer's intelligence. Playing tricks on your customer to get them to sign up or buy a few extra items will only diminish their trust. For example, you can catch your target customer's attention by adding a link claiming a "free trial" – but if he finds out he must pay to sign up before he is eligible for the trial period, the customer is more likely to log out of your page and not return.

Creating an Eye-Catching Logo

Logos are also powerful and influential tools, with children as young as three capable of becoming brand conscious, simply because they can recognize the logo of their favorite product before they can even read. A study conducted by the University of Michigan found that children aged between three to six years of age could not only match products to their logos, they also had very strong views about whether they preferred McDonalds or Burger King, Coca Cola, or Pepsi.

The most powerful logo of all time is said to be Nike's iconic Swoosh, first designed in 1971. The brand name was inspired by Nike, the Greek goddess of victory, so the designer, who was initially only paid $35 for her design, created the Swoosh to indicate speed and movement. While the original design has been modified a few times, it is now so recognizable that in 1995 Nike confidently removed the actual brand name from the logo, leaving the Swoosh to stand alone.

Simplicity is a key element of a successful logo. Apple Computer's first logo, created in 1976, was a detailed 19th century style ink drawing of Sir Isaac Newton sitting under a tree, an apple gleaming above his head. Around the border of the image is a Wordsworth quote: "Newton… a mind forever voyaging through strange seas of thought… alone." While this image probably did connect the name of the company with its philosophy and inspiration, it was far too intricate and old-fashioned and it was not eye catching enough for the message to translate easily in one glance.

So, a year later, another designer tried another approach and created the now-iconic apple symbol, with a bite out of the side so people wouldn't mistake it for a cherry. The original Apple logo was rainbow striped, until the late 1990s when it was changed to monochrome. The company was struggling financially, so Jobs and his team wanted to capitalize on their world-famous logo by making it more prominent on all their products and the enlarged rainbow Apple was expensive to print and didn't complement the products as effectively as the monochrome version.

Sometimes your product name becomes your logo. Coca Cola's iconic logo dates back to 1887, when the designer simply wrote out the name of the product in the most common font at the time. In 1893, the logo's color changed from black to red, and then in 1940 the font was refined to the logo we still see today.

Your Customer's Reticular Activation System (RAS)

No matter how clever and eye-catching your logo, you won't attract everyone's attention. The human brain is programmed with a reticular activation system (RAS) designed to filter visual information based on need, so people will automatically block out whatever is irrelevant. Nobody can absorb every piece of visual information they are exposed to each day. This is why you stop at the traffic lights while driving, although you won't notice which shops you drive past.

Your brain will trigger a "reticular activation" alert if you have a heightened awareness of a particular product or topic. This is why you suddenly see clones of your new car when you take it for the first drive, or you will be more aware of security advertisements after a burglary at your home.

Until the advent of social media, advertisers had no way of harnessing the power of reticular activation. You can't make a potential client subconsciously want your product, in order to stimulate their awareness of your logo. However, social media content development is attuned to your interests and preferences, so if you Google your ideal vacation destination, there's a strong chance a few tourism companies will soon be displaying their advertisements on your computer screen.

When promoting your own products online, remember that the reticular activation system is particularly sensitive to movement, so videos have greater impact than still pictures. If you want to keep your budget low, try a GIF with one point of movement on the screen for extra effect. This type of GIF, known as a cinemograph, has been called the "new wave of advertising." For example, one cinemograph advertisement for a New York bar, shows a still photo of the bar with the image of a yellow taxicab seen in the reflection of the glass moving across the screen, highlighting the bar's name repeatedly as the image loops back to the start.

Promoting Your Brand

Your brand and your brand message should be prominent in all your business-related communications, from your product logos to your web content. Your message should be consistent with your brand, your product, and your professional behavior so you maintain credibility and professional integrity. This clear consistent message will ensure your brand becomes recognizable on the market, building brand equity through trust and repeat business. Your business will promote itself through the reputation of your recognizable brand.

Personal Branding - Dressing for Success

As the living embodiment of your brand, you should ensure that the way your personal appearance and approach reflects the professionalism that your customers expect of your brand. No matter what market you are targeting, your brand should represent energy, expertise and perfectionism.

People make their opinion of you based on three elements: your verbal communication, your tone and manner, and your visual presentation – what you say, how you say it and how you look when you say it. You might think that your speaking manner and dress code are not so important when you have a clear positive brand message to promote your business.

However, according to the Mehrabian Rule, established after a 1967 study, *what* you say is actually the least influential out of the three elements. So, if you deliver your sure-fire brand message in a sullen mumble without making eye contact with your target customer, the customer will not be swayed by the features and benefits of your product. If you are untidy or sloppily dressed, your target customer will see this carelessness as an extension of your business and you will lose credibility. However, if you are smartly dressed in a well-fitted outfit that complements your brand message, and if you can engage your target customer through body language and speaking manner, they will be more intrigued by your central message.

The "Universal Effects of Image"
Your target customer is not the only person affected by how you present yourself. Your perception of your physical appearance will directly affect your confidence and self-esteem and this in turn will affect your speaking manner. A few simple measures, like establishing a "uniform" for work, researching the right fit and style for your body type and a simple grooming routine will help you feel focused and keep your presentation polished. Having a specific "uniform" – a set of clothes designated for work – helps keep you organized and focused. This eliminates the constant question of "what should I wear to work today?" You know what you are wearing, you know that

it is comfortable and appropriate and it is ready. You can purchase a few variations of your uniform, so you have a consistent look in keeping with your brand message.

The Power of Color

Color is a powerful way to keep your brand distinct and identifiable, and you can use color to tie together all the different platforms of your brand. I always dress my brand by wearing a suit with a purple shirt, black suit coat and black dress pants. In the language of colors, purple signifies power, luxury, ambition, and wealth, partly because it is rarely found in nature. It is also associated with spirituality, imagination, and magic. Purple is a blend of blue, which signifies stability, and red which symbolizes energy and passion.

You can match your own brand message to significant or relevant colors. Yellow signifies happiness, warmth, optimism and intellectual energy; a flash of yellow will instantly attract attention and evoke a positive response. However, it is not a good fit for luxury items or safety products.

Green is associated with nature, growth, healing and financial security so it is a good color to use in relation to health, safety, and financial products.

Blue is associated with tranquility, cleanliness and sincerity – while it is currently labelled a "male" color, blue was originally the color designated for baby girls because it was peaceful and calm, while pink was the "boy" color as it was considered more passionate and energetic. It has a good brand association with purifying products, water products or airline services.

However, blue does not have a good connection with food products.

Red is the color of fire and blood, so it is associated with life and heat or passion. It can be used to convey urgency, energy or danger, as well as sexuality and romance.

Orange is a warm invigorating color with a positive connection to food products and outdoor activity. It can be used to attract attention, without having the same urgency as its base colors red and yellow.

White is associated with purity and hygienic cleanliness, and is a very good fit for medical products, charities, and high-tech products.
Black is associated with formality, elegance, and mystery. It is a good brand match for luxury products, but the mysterious connotations can be sinister so it is not a good match for products that rely on trust or optimism.

In Summary
Your *brand* visually and verbally defines your business as unique and distinctive, so you stand out from your competition and build brand equity.

Brand equity is the tangible value of your brand, based on the recognition and loyalty of your growing customer base. Your *brand message* reflects your company values and practices. Your *brand strategy* outlines how you will promote your message within the parameters of your company values.
Your *logo* is the visual representation of your brand message,

and your *slogan* is a catchy verbal summary of your brand message.

Your *personal branding* should extend to your personal appearance, speaking manner and body language.

Once you have established your brand and started to build brand equity, you are ready to start driving sales.

Chapter 5 - To Sell Is Not to Sell

Driving sales can be the most difficult and challenging aspects of your business. Many people have a fear of selling, because they take it personally when the customer does not want to buy from them. You can overcome this fear of rejection by putting it into a professional context: either you are focusing on a prospect who has no interest in your product, or you have the right prospect but they are not ready to buy right now.

When you follow the principles, we discuss in this chapter, you will work out how to identify the right prospect for your product and service, and how to maintain contact with the prospect so they come back to buy from you when they are ready to buy.

A defined sales process is absolutely essential if your business can sustain duplicable results and optimize the process to generate more sales. The key to your sales process is to meet your prospect's needs by providing the necessary solutions to their problems and educating them on what they should look for when buying the products and services you offer. By offering educational opportunities you help your prospects make informed decisions on what they need to buy – and most importantly, they should make the informed decision to buy from YOU.

The three components of a solid sales process are listening, confidence, and education. When you incorporate these components into your approach, you will dramatically increase your sales and profitability. I have seen hundreds of people talk themselves out of a sale by talking about themselves rather than listening to the prospect in order to determine what the prospect needs. When you listen to the prospect, you can pick up on the cues they provide and you will find that the prospect always tells you whether you can close them and how you can close them.

I am a big "systems guy." I help my clients create franchise type systems in their businesses so they work less and earn more money. If they choose to franchise their business, they are already prepared to go that direction. Remember that business is about building relationships and profit is the result of helping people. Speak to the prospect confidently and respectfully. Never interrupt them when they are speaking. Ask open ended questions that give you the answers you need to qualify the prospect and see if they are the right fit for your business.

A sales process is one of the most important processes to implement into your business. Your sales process should be repeatable and measurable so you can assess and improve your results. With a defined sales process, you can spend less money on marketing and advertising while dramatically increasing your sales and profitability at the same time. Yet one of the key factors I see in businesses is a lack of sales process, leading to resources such as time and potential leads being wasted or lost.

To simplify the creation of the sales process, I like to use a system called the "B.E.E.P." process, sometimes also known as the conversion equation. When you have a defined sales process for products and services that are in demand and properly marketed, you can double, triple or even achieve a 5x increase in sales. When you consider that so many companies fail to establish any type of sales process, you can gain a significant advantage over your competition by establishing a defined sales process that allows you to leverage your time and talent by teaching the process to other people.

Why the "Hard Sell" Doesn't Work

One of the biggest obstacles undermining your confidence is the myth that the "hard sell" is the only proven way to drive sales. In fact, the opposite is true. Your customers want to feel they have *chosen* the right product for their needs and that they are making this decision, based on their own good judgement. Salesmen who use the "hard sell" approach tend to minimize the importance of the customer's judgement by telling the customer what he wants. They are trying to bamboozle the customer into making a decision without weighing up the pros and cons.

So, if you are not comfortable with the "hard sell," remember your customer is generally not comfortable with it either. Salespeople who use the hard sell or who rely on NLP tactics to push you to buy also tend to have the highest return rate or customer complaints over other salespeople in their organization. Your best approach is to educate your prospects on what they should look for when looking to buy your products and services. By educating your prospects, you earn their trust and their business.

What is the B.E.E.P. system?

The B.E.E.P. system is the game changer for your business, defining a proven sales process that will enable you to target the right customers, and follow through to create a successful and growing customer platform.

The B.E.E.P. system has four key components – BUILD an audience; ENGAGE their attention; EDUCATE them about what they need; and finally PROMOTE a low-risk offer that will encourage them to become a customer/client.

Build an Audience

Your "audience" is your platform of prospects – potential and repeat customers who will potentially purchase your products and services. Your business relies on your ability to find potential customers so you can continue increasing your sales. A strong prospecting strategy enables you to build a solid customer base while providing a range of avenues to continue connecting with new prospects. There are five main sources for prospects:

Referrals: The concept of your customers referring you to their network seems like an effortless way to increase your customer platform. However, if you really want to power up your referrals, you need to give your customers a reason to talk about you.

The classic way to encourage referrals is to offer your customers an incentive to recommend you – give them a fridge magnet or a calendar, and they will have your contact details on hand if anybody asks. Give them a VIP voucher or a discount for introducing a friend, and they may dutifully introduce one more customer in order to collect their prize.

Another more-subtle strategy is to tell your customers engaging anecdotes that are easily repeated and all end with the same moral to the story – you solved another customer's problem. For example, a real estate agent could tell customers a story about the advice he gave a couple who were conflicted about the sale of a house during a divorce. A caterer could talk about how he navigated the challenge of catering for a wedding reception when the power went out in the kitchen. Your customer will remember these stories and find opportunities to repeat them in conversation. Their listener will, in turn, see you as someone who can solve their immediate problem or resolve their stress about an upcoming event.

Networking: The key to successful networking is to approach each networking event as an opportunity to help people. Learn to engage with each conversation, take an interest in what your new acquaintance does for a living, and practice active listening while they explain their challenges and triumphs. When you show interest and respect, the other person will reciprocate and be more responsive if you offer any solutions to their problems. Don't "hard sell" your solutions – your business isn't necessarily the right answer at this point.

Unsuccessful networkers are those who are looking for a solution to their own problems – they want someone to hire them or employ them, so all their conversations are focused on getting the other person to help them. This approach reveals an underlying desperation and lack of confidence. Your goal at a networking event is not to secure a sale, it is to build your network without any ulterior motive. This involves being friendly, open, receptive, and helpful. Maintain the communication by exchanging business cards and sending a courteous email the next day.

Direct Marketing: While direct mail was once a key promotional strategy for businesses, it is now found to be too expensive as it doesn't generate the same level of return as other technologies, such as Ringless Voicemail and Voice Broadcast whose direct response lead generation is proven to work in over 50 different industries. In my experience, they are particularly effective for doctors, restaurants, non-profits, political campaigns, and debt collectors.

Ringless voicemail campaigns have a higher response rate than other forms of direct marketing, partly because from the prospect's point of view, they are convenient and unobtrusive. The prospect isn't interrupted during dinner by a phone call or a knock at the door. They can read the message when it suits them and consider the offer without any pressure, which makes them more likely to be in a responsive frame of mind.

If your company is targeting the consumer market, Ringless Voicemail is a simple and cost-effective way to generate new business. It is structured to work like direct mail, once you identify the area code, zip code, or city where you want to deliver your message. You record a voicemail message for your prospects, inviting them to call you or visit your business.

Voice Broadcast is structured to market your business products and services to other businesses. You can target your ideal prospects by city, area code, zip code, industry, size of business, and revenue. Your pre-recorded message is delivered to the business after hours, while it is closed.

Purchased email lists: When you purchase an email contact list of contacts fitting the profile of your target customer from a reputable source, you can immediately boost traffic to your site and from there, increase the call-to-action response. Your visibility will also improve as more people become aware of your business and central message even if they are not ready to become customers. I recommend purchasing lead lists for Ringless Voicemail and Voice Broadcast leads. I use <u>List Giant</u>.

Online Prospecting

Your website is also an excellent prospecting tool, although most business owners don't use it effectively. Rather than driving prospects directly to your website, you want to drive them to a lead capture or squeeze page or automated webinar. The "squeeze page" is a landing page designed to capture email addresses and turn visitors into subscribers. Remember, your goal is to educate your prospects through your regular updates. Even the website address on your business cards should be the URL to the squeeze page or to the automated webinar. Your business cards are a lead generation tool when properly constructed.

Your goal is to collect the contact information and relevant background of every visitor, so you can follow up on their visit and build a relationship. The best way to encourage visitors to leave their details is to deliver a free downloadable book, discount voucher, or buyers guide to their inbox. As a bonus, you are presenting yourself as an expert, simply by having this book on hand so you can help the visitor by sharing your expertise.

Once the visitor enters their details, they should be transferred to a simple "Thank you" page that confirms their book (or other free resource) will be in their inbox. At the same time, their contact details have been transferred to your database. From there, you can send pre-written generic emails to your new contact, delivering a clear call-to-action with each message. We will look at how to create compelling email content in the next section on engaging a customer's attention.

Quantify Your Contacts

Not all the names you gather will actually be potential customers. Once you have gathered a promising list of names, you need to quantify the list so you can assess which ones are actually real prospects. You want to construct at least five customer profiles or avatars of your ideal customers. This will help you save time when sorting through your prospects to find the good ones.

When you have a clear profile of your target customers and clients, you will find it easier to focus your attention on those people amongst all your other prospects and contacts. We'll talk more about creating customer profiles or avatars in the next chapter on Marketing. Your chances of success in the sales process will increase if you concentrate on customers that are closer to a "sure thing" rather than wasting your time and energy chasing a customer who is not interested in your product or has a completely different budget in mind. Work through the lists of names that you gather from your sources, and eliminate those names that do not fit the profile of your target customer.

Engage Your Prospect's Attention

Once you have a list of viable prospects, you need to engage their attention so they know that your company is memorable and trustworthy, with the right solution for their needs. The key to engaging with your prospect is to concentrate on what the client wants to achieve rather than what the product can achieve. You are not selling a product to your prospect – you are selling the belief that your product or service can make your prospect's business even better and stronger. You are selling a new improved version of the clients themselves.

The Engaging Message

Many business owners make the fundamental mistake of telling the prospect all about the features and don't spend enough time focusing on the benefits of the product or service – you expect the client to be as excited as you are about this brilliant new innovation. Remember features tell and benefits sell. When you are with a prospect, you will only be talking 10 to 20% of the time and listening 80 to 90% of the time. So why doesn't this sales technique work?

When you talk about the product or service, you are focusing too much of your time talking about yourself and the features of the product, rather than listening to the prospect and answering questions to explain how your product or service will solve their specific problem. The prospect wants the assurance of knowing that the product or service they purchase from you will solve their problem. Rather than telling the client what you have achieved by creating your business, tell them what they can achieve and how the product will solve the problem they are having. (Remember you were listening when you were talking to the prospect. You know exactly what their problem is, if you can solve it and how you can solve it.)

The client is on the verge of ultimate success and fulfilment, with just one specific problem holding them back – and your product will solve that problem, giving the prospect the confidence of knowing their problem will be solved when they purchase the product or service from you. After the purchase, you will remain alongside the customer every step of the way through your customer service and follow up to ensure the customer is happy with their purchase.

Engaging on Social Media

It is important that you pick the right social media networks for acquiring new customers. Facebook, LinkedIn, or Twitter are excellent places to start engaging with your prospects. The secret to using social media platforms effectively is to work out how to tailor your brand message to the unique style and message of each platform. It is also wise to set a specific timeframe and routine for your social media engagement to ensure your message stays on point and you don't become so caught up in maintaining your social media identity that you forget to engage in the real business at hand. At the end of the day your social media engagement should attract customers, not just "likes" and "shares."

Facebook

With more than 1 billion users, Facebook is sure to connect you with your target customers, so you can promote your business on a relaxed and informal platform. Start a conversation with your customers, learn how they feel about your products or services, and start a competition so they share your posts with their friends.

LinkedIn

LinkedIn is a social networking site for professionals who can connect with contacts or potential contacts to build their own unique and expansive network. Your LinkedIn profile outlines your career in a similar style to a detailed resume, with the added benefit of including personal recommendations and endorsements from colleagues, clients, and industry peers. You can also engage in group discussions and post blogs, articles, and advertisements on the LinkedIn forum. Your LinkedIn profile has the potential to give a comprehensive view of your experience, expertise, customer interaction, management skills, and team leadership abilities.

Google+

Google+ has become the Internet's fastest growing social network and it has excellent resources for professional networking. Create a Google Plus profile with a professional photograph or branded image, along with a link to your other social media platforms, including your website, blog, Facebook, and Twitter.

One of the unique advantages of Google+ is that you can categorize your connections into separate interlinking networks called Circles. This helps you keep a handle on maintaining a consistent and relevant message for separate audiences - your message to existing customers would be modified for prospects while your professional updates would be completely different to the personal updates you would send to people in your Family/Friends Circle. You can engage in productive group discussions with members of your network as well as sharing and commenting on the latest posted content.

YouTube

YouTube is one of the world's most popular search engines and it is a powerful promotional tool that provides a dynamic extra dimension to your brand. If you feel that your brand is suited to a video promotion, then YouTube is the best platform for that video. If you want your YouTube video to work as an advertisement, remember that most people skip the video after the first five or ten seconds, so make those seconds count!

Instagram

Instagram is another social media tool with the potential for great impact on your target customer. Your Instagram account can develop its own "personality" offering a unique view of the world through the perspective of your brand's vision and mission, inspiring your audience to select your product or services and appreciate what you contribute to the community. Build and expand your following by connecting your Facebook account to Instagram and using relevant hashtags to spread your images around to other pages. Create your own branded hashtag so your images will always stay connected to your brand and your business. Plan ahead about what you intend to post so you update your account regularly and retain a consistent and professional visual image. Keep your target audience engaged by telling the story of your brand through your pictures and occasionally alternating the strong branded images with relevant fun images, so viewers will want to keep following your account to find out "what happens next." Actively follow other relevant accounts by liking and commenting on their images. Set up competitions to encourage active engagement from your followers.

Pinterest

Pinterest is another form of visual marketing through social media. This platform actively encourages followers to share images far more actively than Facebook or Instagram. You will need to tailor your brand message around Pinterest's central message of visual marketing to promote an aspirational lifestyle through inspiring, creative, and innovative images.

Tumblr

Tumblr is a microblogging site that is extremely popular with younger audiences and works best with businesses such as fashion, food, and publishing/broadcast media. You can combine images and brief blocks of newsworthy text in a more versatile and creative way than other platforms. The purpose of a Tumblr post is to help draw viewers to your other platforms or even to close the sale. For example, the Kmart Tumblr presents coupons for viewers to redeem at the store, while other companies use Tumblr to draw viewers to their Instagram or to the latest article on their online magazine.

Vine

Vine is a mobile app that helps you create six-second looping videos which you can share on Twitter and Facebook. These videos can be the basis for engaging in conversation with your followers or they can work as a brief promotion for one of your products or display your work for a recent client. You can even encourage your followers to post their own video promoting your product for you.

Snapchat

Snapchat is an instant messaging site which delivers "Snapchat Stories" consisting of a string of snaps which combine to make a video narrative. These stories last online for 24 hours and they are intended to be "private" for the immediate followers only. They are most suited for providing access to live events or giving followers a sneak preview of a new product. You can also engage your Snapchat community by setting up competitions and promotions for their eyes only.

Unlike traditional promotional forums, social media sites such as your website and Facebook page give your prospects the opportunity to tell you directly what they want from your product or service. This way, you can tailor your promotions – or even your product – to meet the expectations of your target audience as you can find out what appeals to them about your product or service, and what needs are driving them to seek your product.

Visual content is an essential element of your social media. Your visual content must reflect your brand message consistently and strongly across every platform. Viewers form their first impression of a website within half a second, yet it can be much more difficult to change that first impression. Make sure all your photographic images fit your branding message, to keep your brand memorable and authentic.

Make your social media as friendly and interactive as possible, by inviting visitors to comment on blogs, participate in surveys or – if it suits your business model – sharing photos on Instagram. Create incentives such as discounts or bonus vouchers to encourage them to sign up to the website. If your social media sites are interesting and engaging to visit with plenty of fresh content and opportunities for conversation, you will find that your content is shared and promoted, expanding your network.

When setting up your website, remember that not all your visitors will enter your site through the home page, as they could be redirected to another page through a link in an article or blog. So, make sure each page clearly promotes your key message and your call to action.

Creating Downloadable Content

As we discussed in the previous section, you can engage prospects by providing free downloadable content on your website. This content should be compelling and intriguing to your target customer, and it should have an attention-grabbing headline to encourage them to download *now*. Make your headline ultra-specific and urgent with a definite promise to your prospect. There are a few strategies for writing the perfect headline (https://www.enchantingmarketing.com/headline-formulas/).

The Million-Dollar Question Formula

What is the million-dollar question your prospects are struggling to answer? Research shows that question headlines attract more clicks than other headlines, simply because your target audience wants to find out the answer to that million-dollar question.

Some successful examples of effective question headlines are:
"Is Brand a Google Ranking Factor?"
"Fat Shaming vs Body Acceptance: Is it okay to be fat?"
"How much do Keywords Still Matter?"

The How-To Formula

A "How To" headline promises to provide a simple step-by-step solution to your prospect's most insurmountable problem. The formula is most effective when the problem is particularly specific. Some "How To" examples are:

"How to Prepare for a Customer Meeting"
"How to Negotiate a Better Home Loan Interest Rate"
"How to Attract and Retain Customers"

The Guide Formula

Like the previous examples, the "guide" headline offers a simple answer to an overwhelming problem. The reader is assured this comprehensive handbook will guide him through every aspect of the issue. Remember to state the type of guide, such as the Compact Guide or the Beginner's Guide or the Scientific Guide, so the target reader will have that added reassurance that this guide is tailored to his needs, is authoritative, and easy to follow.

Some "Guide" examples are:

"The Beginner's Guide to Investing in Stocks"
"The Small Business Guide to Increasing Profits"
"The Creative Guide to Building Your Network"

The "List" Formula

The List generally has a number in the title – "8 Reasons why" or "Top 10 Solutions to" so above all else it offers a range of snapshot solutions – it promises not to be too in-depth and complex, with just a paragraph or two on every option.

There are a few variations of the "List" formula, such as the "Error List" and the "Reasons Why List." Readers are attracted to the Error List, because it tells them what NOT to do, giving them the reassurance that they can avoid simple yet common errors. Examples include "Top 5 Mistakes New Investors Make" or "9 SEO Mistakes that make you lose business."The "Reasons Why List" tells the reader why they should take a certain action – "Five Reasons Why Daily Exercise is Good for Business."

Engaging in Person

When you meet a prospect for the first time, they will instantly form an opinion of your expertise, your trustworthiness, and your relatability. The key question in their mind is: Can this person solve my problems? They are more likely to answer "Yes" if you can demonstrate that you are friendly, communicative, knowledgeable, and a good listener. The best way to convey all this is to be relaxed and extremely well prepared!

Your first customer meeting has the potential to be extremely valuable and productive with every one-hour meeting having the potential to draw multiple sources of income for months and years to come. So, it is worth investing time into preparing thoroughly so you make the best possible first impression.

Preparing for Your First Meeting

Research the background of your customer and their company by reading their website, learning their vision and mission, and checking LinkedIn profiles for additional information about their background and perspective. When you have a clear understanding of your target customer, you can tailor your approach specifically to their needs and expectations. This background information will save you valuable time during the meeting, as you can go straight to solving the customer's current problem.

Also research their history with your own company as this information will shape your approach. A first-time customer will need a different approach than an established customer who wants to expand their business. If they have previously been unhappy with your service, you can show them how you intend to address the past problems so your service will improve this time around.

Outline an agenda for the meeting by making a list of the items you wish to discuss, and the outcome you wish to achieve. You could send a copy of your agenda to the customer in case they want to add a few more items to the discussion list – this also shows them that you are dedicated to helping them.

Your customer would have done their own research and may have some reservations about some aspects of your service. Make sure you are prepared enough to anticipate these objections, so you can give a positive and reassuring response.

No matter how carefully you research in advance, you should always assume you have missed something of vital importance. So, make a note on your personal meeting agenda to conclude the meeting by saying: "Before we finish, do you have any questions or concerns about what we talked about today?" This gives the prospect the opportunity to express any concerns or reservations so you can offer reassurance before you start work. You should keep the first meeting to less than 15 minutes and stay focused on getting to know the customer and understand their needs. Do not try to pitch them in the first meeting.

Remember the Golden Rule:
Business is about building relationships. Profit is the result of helping people. It can take 5 to 12 touch points with a prospect before they are willing to buy from you.

Your Customer Approach
There are a number of different customer approaches that will help build a rapport with your customer and demonstrate your expertise.

The product approach involves giving your customer a sample of your product. This approach enables the customer to try the product, allowing the customer to make an informed choice. This approach is particularly popular in the food industry and cosmetic industry, and it is a good way to encourage customers to expand their use of your products.

The premium approach involves giving the customer a gift, preferably a branded novelty such as branded pens or calendars. Another customer approach is to ask a leading question, so you can engage the customer in a conversation about your product and identify their core needs. For example, if you are trying to win the customer over from a rival, you could ask "What do you like best about your current supplier? What don't you like?" Alternately you could ask about their business plans, by asking "What are your short-term goals and long-term goals?" or "What do you like best about your current system?" Questions such as these give you the opportunity to encourage the customer to be actively involved in the discussion, and show that you are interested in securing the best outcome for the customer.

Educate Your Prospects

Today's customers are extremely well-informed, with a wealth of material available to them on every subject. This means that your prospects have their own set ideas, based on their general knowledge and personal experience, about the benefits of your products or services in relation to the competition. Basic marketing strategies are not effective in the face of established opinions – the prospect has already either decided for or against you.

So, your best strategy is to educate your prospects by providing them with information in the form of webinars, videos and audios that are easy for them to access to learn more about you, your products, or services. If you have thoroughly qualified your prospects, you are educating someone who has a need for your product and shares your fundamental philosophy. Now you have to educate them so they can see clearly for themselves that you are the right company to provide the product or service they need, in keeping with their philosophy.

Customers who are drawn to your philosophy will become more knowledgeable through the additional information you provide, and this in turn will increase their trust in your expertise and their respect for your personal brand.

The following websites demonstrate how educating your customers can strengthen and consolidate your brand.

Ethical Jeweler Australia (EJA)
The name of this company clearly explains its philosophy – the jewelry is designed from recycled precious metals and stones to reduce the environmental impact of mining and support human rights. In the web content, founder Melinda Nugent explains that mining for gold, silver, and platinum is an extremely destructive process, while the extraction process makes use of highly toxic metals; in some countries the mining industry is also strongly associated with human exploitation and child labor.

The EJA website not only outlines all the global benefits of supporting ethically sources jewelry production, it also provides a free downloadable book entitled *How you can create her dream engagement ring,* educating potential customers on how to design a unique and personal engagement ring setting.

Goulet Pen Company

The Goulet Pen Company specializes in selling unique and beautifully crafted writing instruments, ranging from highlighters and rollerball pens to classic fountain pens and artistic brush pens. Founder Brian Goulet acknowledges that the choice of such a pen is both "personal and physical in nature" so it was challenging to market the writing instruments online when customers don't have the opportunity to try them in person before they make their purchase.

Goulet has bridged this gap in customer knowledge by uploading short videos of himself writing with each new variation of writing instrument. In the video, he tells target customers whether the pen writes finely or firmly, how it feels to hold, how to replace the ink and which ink is the best option for this particular pen. This way customers can make an informed choice before investing in such a personal online purchase.

Promote a Low Risk Offer

You have successfully gone through the first three steps of the B.E.E.P. process – you have BUILT an audience for your business and from here, you have identified your target customers; you have ENGAGED your prospects attention by having multiple touch points with the prospect through social media, voice broadcast, or ringless voicemail, text messages, meetings, email marketing, or telephone calls; and you have EDUCATED them about your product or service, so they are confident they are making an informed choice by giving you their business.

Now it is time to meet the prospect and PROMOTE a low risk offer. If you have followed what we covered in this book, your prospects will start calling you, ready to buy. Set up a 5-minute phone call or coffee meeting, so you can get a feel for where they are at in your sales process, and see if you will be a good fit working together. If you actually arrange this meeting, you are striding ahead of 48% of your competition – according to sales statistics, almost half of all sales people do not make this first meeting with a contact. Yet 80% of sales are made on the fifth to twelfth contact.

This is where marketing and sales automation becomes an important part of your marketing strategy. You can leverage technology to perform those touch points to keep your prospects educated and engaged until they are ready to buy. I'll talk about marketing and sales automation in an upcoming chapter. So, it is certainly an excellent investment to persevere with your prospect and maintaining strong communication so you can finally land the sale. And it all starts with that first brief meeting.

Your Presentation

Your presentation is an important element of the customer approach. Good sales people have two crucial qualities – they are storytellers, who can engage the customers with a narrative, and they are active listeners, who demonstrate that the customer's needs are paramount. People don't buy products or services. People buy YOUR stories. People buy you!

You can create your narrative as part of your presentation, to ensure you are presenting the type of product or service that would fit the customer's needs and budget. By creating a narrative, you capture the customer's imagination and help them visualize how your product or service will improve their life or their business.

Active listening is important for showing the customer that you are interested in hearing their perspective and solving their unique problems – it shows that your concern is for the customer rather than making the sale. With an active listening approach, you are also showing respect for the customer by taking their concerns seriously and giving them your undivided attention. This is your opportunity to address any objections or concerns the customer has about your product or business. If you take these objections seriously and show the customer how you will solve these issues, you will win the customer's trust and confidence.

The presentation is probably the most challenging aspect of the sales process. However, the more effort you put into the previous steps, such as qualifying your customer and preparing for your approach, the easier this process will be.

Discuss Their Concerns
Ask them directly if they have any concerns that are holding them back from working with you. It is possible that the customer is hesitant to close the deal because they still have reservations about some aspects of your business: the financial outlay might be more than they originally budgeted; or the customer may still not be 100% convinced that you can solve their key problem.

When you ask them about their concerns, you are actively demonstrating that their business interests are your priority – you want to provide the right solution for their needs. Once they express their concerns, you can address those concerns directly – show them how the solution is tailored to their needs, or offer a financial incentive such as a bonus offer or a freebie.

Follow Up

Once you have established that your product or service is a good solution for the prospect, and you have thoroughly examined all the customer's concerns, it is highly likely they will still say "No," when you try to close the deal. Only 2% of sales are made on the first contact, 3% on the second contact and 5% on the third contact.

So, if you don't make the sale on the first contact, don't give up hope. Accept that they have said "No" and offer to help them if they should need your services in the future. Don't waste your energy trying to force a "No" into a "Yes" as you have other prospects who need your attention.

However, you can follow up with your prospect again to give them another opportunity to close the deal. Rather than simply "checking in" with monotonous regularity, each follow-up should be an opportunity to provide fresh and targeted offers or information. Send frequent and relevant updates, such as the latest special deal for the product or service of their interest. Don't be afraid to repeat the key information every single time – you want the prospect to stay focused on why this particular product or service is the solution for their problem, while you provide additional information to drive home the sale.

As you regularly follow up with each prospect, use a range of communication techniques, alternating direct mail, email, text and other media. This way, you manage to follow up with each prospect via their preferred media. Keep your customer database "live" so you don't waste opportunities or effort chasing non-existent leads.

Closing the Sale

When your prospect is ready to buy, don't talk them out of the sale and don't be afraid to ask for the sale. Here are a few closing strategies that you can use to help you with closing the sale. If you have been listening to your prospect's needs and concerns, you will know exactly how to move them from a prospect into a new client for your business. Practice listening!

The Alternative Close

When you offer the customer two options, they are instinctively going to select their favored option. Say to the client: "Taking your needs into consideration, I believe these two options are the best fit for you. Which one do you think is the best solution?" This gives the customer the opportunity to independently weigh up the two options – "I like this one best, but I did like the fact that the other one included XYZ." This exercise gives you an extra opportunity to tailor the solution to the customer's needs. And once they have engaged in this level of discussion, they have demonstrated that they are visualizing the product as their solution, so they are ready to close the sale with you.

The Assumptive Close

Move the conversation smoothly from promotion to assuming

the deal is done by saying "So when should we get started?" The customer is arranging dates, planning the start even though they haven't actually signed the project over to you. If you have handled every other aspect of the sale correctly, the customer simply needs encouragement to close the deal; otherwise, they may go away to "think about it" and become distracted by some other aspect of their business or by one of your competitors.

The Deadline Close
Explain that due to time constraints you need the signed contract by a specific date.

The Fear Close
Explain your concern about uncontrollable external factors affecting the customer's business if they don't close today.

The process of navigating a prospect into a customer is not simply a matter of luck – it is a combination of strong research, quantification, presentation, and communication so you are constantly channeling your energy on a range of prospects who have a genuine need for your product or service. The B.E.E.P. system will ensure that you always have new prospects on the horizon while you patiently convert your current prospects into customers.

In Summary
The B.E.E.P. system creates an assembly line of prospects so you are never short of leads. The four steps of the B.E.E.P. system are:

BUILD an audience through networking in your local market, your social media platform, and marketing strategies, so you can sort through your contacts and concentrate on the prospects who are the closest fit to your target customer. Your remaining audience will build your brand recognition and have the potential to become customers in the future. So, your promotional platform should be instantly recognizable to create brand awareness, and should consistently reflect your professionalism, integrity, and expertise. Share your stories with your prospects!

ENGAGE their attention by creating a narrative that drives home the need for your product or service. Tell your prospects a story that shows them how your product or service can create a solution for their specific problem. You need to have correctly identified your prospects in order for the narrative to resonate with them.

EDUCATE your prospects so they can expand and consolidate their understanding of how your solution will work for them. As they are your target market, they will already be drawn to the philosophy behind your business, and additional education will increase their respect for your expertise while strengthening their opinion about your product or service.

PROMOTE your best deal. When you approach your prospect, be prepared to make a strong impression with a tempting offer. Remember that the first approach doesn't generally conclude with an immediate sale, so have a follow-up system in place to keep approaching your customer until the deal is closed.

This is where your marketing strategy comes into play, as we will discuss in the next chapter.

Chapter 6 - Modern Marketing

"Marketing" has become a rather abstract term – you know that you need marketing for your business, and you might even decide that you need a big budget for marketing. But what are you planning to achieve?

The key to marketing is understanding the problems that your market is facing, and delivering a message to your market that spurs them to take action. You need to send a message to your market, saying you understand their pain and struggles and you have the solution to their problems.

The earliest marketing experts were the street sellers who would call out: "Get your fresh apples here! Crisp red apples, only ten cents a dozen!" The target customer knew where to find the apple seller and they were drawn to the price and quality even if they hadn't thought of wanting apples until they heard the seller.

Later during the era of television and glossy magazines, marketing became synonymous with advertising. Companies could set up a huge budget for advertising, and purchase some high-profile ad space… and hope for the best. Of the millions of people dozing in front of the television or flipping through a magazine, a certain percentage of them would fit the parameters of your target audience; and of those, some of them would have noticed the advertisement and decided to act upon it. The best strategy was to ensure that the ads were so catchy and memorable, they built brand recognition beyond the target audience, so that customers knew where to find you when they wanted you.

Now we are in a new era of marketing, where we have the tools to direct our advertising straight to the target audience. Marketing is a more complex term, relating to the creation of a story that presents and defines your brand. Just as an advertisement's catchy jingle can define a product, a visually compelling image coupled with an engaging story can define your brand through marketing.

In this chapter, we look at how to define your marketing role and your goals, and I will show you strategies to create a self-sustaining marketing system for your business, so your customers promote and expand your customer platform on your behalf.

Your Marketing Role

It is important to understand the scope and limitations of marketing your brand. First let's look at what is NOT part of your marketing responsibility.

Someone else creates the product or service with all its features; someone else produces and distributes the product or delivers the services; someone else sets the price according to the costs involved in creation and distribution. When you are running a small business of course, you could easily take ownership of all these responsibilities as well as marketing the brand, but it is extremely important to understand that these are SEPARATE responsibilities to marketing.

If you confuse your marketing role with production, distribution, or price setting, you might be tempted to keep altering the product to meet the demands of your perceived target customer. As marketing expert, your job is to find the actual target customer – the person seeking these benefits to solve their particular problem within the price bracket of your brand.

As the marketing manager for your brand, your role starts when you take that first fresh look at the complete packaged product or service. In marketing, we talk of the "4 Ps" which are: product, pricing, positioning, and placement. These are basically the four compass points you need to identify that will help you navigate the product to the target market.

The product of course, is the central point in the equation – without the product, you would have no business and no target market. So, look at the product's features and benefits, and all its variables. What are the selling points and who wants these features and benefits to fill a need in their lives?

Once you start considering who wants the product, you can look at pricing. Your target market may be budget conscious or status conscious. If they are budget conscious, you can promote an expensive product as a long-term practical investment; if they are prepared to pay a higher price, you can promote the product as a luxury status item. Where can you find this target customer and how can you present this product/service in order to appeal to the target customer most effectively?

When you have established the pricing for the product, you can look at how you are positioning it in relation to the competition. You could promote your product as better than the current leading brand, a cheaper or more efficient alternative to the leading brand, or so different from the leader that it is whole new product.

Identifying Your Target Customer
When you are selling a product or service that everybody needs – for example, if you are a doctor promoting your medical care your marketing strategy simply involves publicizing your name, address, and business hours throughout your local area, so when people need you, they can find you. When you are selling a *want,* you must find a way to create a connection with your target customer because you are not out to reach everyone – you must target the person who wants your product.

However, it is also useful to create a sense of need around your product. Nobody truly needs a diamond ring, but De Beer's Jewelers created one of the most successful advertising campaigns in history with the slogan: "A Diamond is forever." Suddenly, every engaged couple "needed" to prove their eternal love by purchasing a diamond engagement ring.

Today, storage is currently a top-selling product range based purely on the chasm between *want* and *need.* People want more consumer items than they can store in their homes, so rather than throwing excess items away, they "need" to purchase storage units so they can keep the clutter tidy. Find a way to promote your product or service as something your target customer needs, even if it is a luxury item.

You will find it easier to connect with customers and new email subscribers if you create a customer avatar identifying your ideal customer. By creating an avatar, you can ensure that your message is direct, relevant, and resonates with your target customer every time. A customer avatar is compiled as a composite of your ideal customer, to create an individual with a name, a picture, and specific demographic. Your avatar has all the characteristics and perspectives of your ideal customer, so you can target all your marketing messages to this one specific "person."

So how do you make an avatar? Start by researching all you can about your target customer, based on what you can learn from face-to-face meetings and online interactions. Make note of their social and cultural environment, their values, their emotional responses, their demographic – age, sex, marital status, income – and even their speaking manner. Make a list of all the common traits you can identify, and use this list to create your avatar. Give your avatar a name, an age, a job and a family – you can even decide what your avatar looks like based on your research!

Write a short autobiographical sketch of your avatar to ensure that everyone in your organization knows exactly the person they are targeting.

For example:
My name is Steve and I am 45 years old. I work 50 hours a week in a senior management role and I travel several times a year for work. I take pride in providing my wife and children with a high standard of living and I want my children to have the best possible education, regardless of cost. My main challenge in life is time-management as I

have so many different calls upon my time. I'm extremely organized and competitive, at work and when I play sports on the weekends. I enjoy watching team sports but prefer individual competition that combines networking, like golf. I'm always looking for ways to improve my golf game.

Steve's lifestyle, demographic and goals based on this character sketch also gives a good insight into his worldview – his values, opinions, and expectations based on how he sees the world.

What is your target customer's worldview?

Your worldview is based on the biases and expectations you have established in your mind, based on your experience and observation of the world. People instinctively resist changing their worldview, although it is possible to shift someone's worldview. In marketing, you can work within the parameters of a target customer's worldview and shift it slightly if necessary. For example, McDonalds is renowned as an icon of the fast food industry. The worldview of McDonald's is that it is fast, convenient, cheap, family-friendly… and unhealthy.

For those customers who value the convenience and the low price for a family meal, the unhealthy aspect of McDonald's wasn't initially an issue. As the unhealthy aspect of fast food became more dominant in people's worldview, McDonald's lost customers so they started introducing healthy options and healthier promotional practices. However, these changes did not make much positive impact on sales as people could not overlook their worldview that food from McDonald's was unhealthy. Customers who choose to go to McDonald's still tend to be drawn to the unhealthy options!

Bottled water is an example of a successful shift in worldview. At one time, it would have been laughable to consider selling bottled water when people can simply fill their own bottles at home. But as the soda industry grew bigger, the health message that sodas were overloaded with sugar took hold of the target audience. People wanted to cut down on soda, and at the same time, articles were being published telling people they needed to drink 8 glasses of water a day to stay hydrated. The soda companies diversified their product and started selling bottled water, creating a lucrative new industry.

When you know your target customer's worldview, you can align your marketing message with their vision for themselves and their lifestyle. Some customers will be focused on safety above all else, others will be focused on adventure, some are looking for convenience, others are looking for eco-friendly solutions, some will be looking for a practical budget product, and others are looking for something aspirational. All of them want to feel that you offer value for their money, according to their standards and their worldview.

Whoever your target customer is, you will have to start by shifting their worldview of business promotion in general – today's customer is over-loaded with advertising and promises, so they tend to be cynical about marketing strategies. So, your first task is to build their trust and ensure they believe that your company shows integrity and honesty. Only promise what you can deliver because false promises are fatal to your credibility.

Creating Your Narrative

You know your target customer, and you have established a position for your brand. Now you need an authentic brand story that will resonate with your target audience and link back to your product. The key words here are *authentic, resonate,* and *link.*

An *authentic* story promotes values that you uphold in every aspect of your brand. For example, a popular brand story today is "environmentally friendly." You can write a strong compelling story about how environmentally friendly your product/service is and this will draw a great target market. But what happens if your production practices or source materials don't match your message? You lose credibility. Look at the values behind your brand and promote these genuine values as an integral part of your brand.

You can make your brand *resonate* with your customer by inspiring emotion through your message. Do you want your customer to feel romantic, motivated, affluent, empowered, or even afraid? Inspire the emotion that matches their need, and they will see your brand as the best way to express or fulfill their emotional need.

The brand message will also resonate with your customer if you highlight familiar concerns or situations, helping the target customer visualize the brand *linking* with their everyday life, and as a solution to their everyday concerns. Your target customers should be able to fit themselves into your story – they can see themselves driving the car you are selling, or eating the pasta, or wearing the jacket.

Your product or service should fit into their image of who they want to be and what they want to achieve. Of course, you need to know your target audience in order to create the right story. About twenty years ago, many advertisers faced a backlash from consumers because they were marketing cooking ingredients and household appliances to the quintessential 1950s housewife, whose goal in life was to have a perfectly tidy house and a decent meal on the table when her husband came home from work.

It took a while for women to convince advertisers that they actually resented this story. Advertisers had to create a different story to acknowledge that women were financially independent with ambitions beyond household duties. Once this new story was acknowledged and embraced, companies found they needed to refine their products to allow for the fact that women were occupied with diverse interests and responsibilities. Now anyone promoting household products would position themselves as providing no-fuss quick and easy convenience.

Ultimately, you want your story to inspire a sense of familiarity and trust. Your target customer should see that you are familiar with their values, needs, and fears, and they trust that your brand will solve their problems. Even before you land the first sale, when your target customer recognizes your name, and associates it with trust, they are more drawn to your products. Your brand story should make a promise to your target customer and to your team. Promise your customers that the product will deliver a certain result, which will be a solution to their key problem.

At the same time, promise your team and yourself that you will unite the product with its target market. Make sure the promise is deliverable and then work towards exceeding expectations.

Another benefit to trust is that you have already established open communication through a range of platforms. Next time you launch a product, you just need to notify your existing audience, because they've been waiting to hear from you!

Establishing Your Platform

As I mentioned earlier, it was not easy to monitor marketing results through traditional advertising platforms such as glossy magazines and television advertisements. These platforms certainly had the ability to build brand awareness beyond your target audience, but how strongly did they impact on the behavior of your target audience? You were spending big money on an unknown result.

Today, you can measure the impact of the platforms you use for promoting your brand and this gives you an important insight into where you should invest your most valuable resources – your time and your money. Whatever platform or platforms you use, you want to see results. Time and money are both of value here. Just as traditional advertisers threw good money after glossy ads that didn't necessarily bring results, today's marketing teams can spend fruitless hours on social media, answering queries, and posting photos – essentially marketing the product, but not necessarily getting the value back in responses.

Whatever platforms or strategies you use to promote your

business, you need to find a way to monitor and measure their progress. What can you change? Internally, you may have some opportunity to change the product. Externally, you can change the customer's perception/create new market. Invest your money wisely – make sure you see results.

Measure the results for each platform so you can be confident that the return exceeds the input. Nurture your platforms so you audience will start working for you, promoting your business to friends and associates, and sharing your results.

Create a Self-Sustaining Marketing Strategy

So far, we have talked about how to establish a marketing strategy by building a social media platform that will attract potential customers. Now we are going to look at how to make this platform self-sustaining by establishing strategies that will ensure your customer base promotes your business on your behalf.

Four Stages of Self-Sustained Marketing

The first stage is to trigger a sense of "want." You can promote a preview of a new item, creating a hunger in the customer to try this item. The second stage is to shift their thinking, and create a new perception, so they have a sense of needing the new product. Thirdly, you make the customer contact you, by responding to an email or a social media post. The fourth and final step is to get them to share your message with others; again, social media is instrumental here, as they can share a post or tag friends.

This strategy is a cyclical process, where you are

The Consistency Principle

Humans have an overriding need to maintain a law of consistency in our thoughts, words, and actions. When you show an inconsistency between your words and your actions, people tend to accept your actions as the truth rather than your words. This is important for you to remember when you create a key marketing message that resonates with your target customer's worldview – as I mentioned earlier, if your behavior deviates from your message, you will quickly lose credibility with your target audience.

However, the consistency principle is also a useful marketing concept, as you can ask your customers to demonstrate their loyalty through a small action or by accepting a small request. For example, if you send out a marketing email with two options – "Click YES if you want our free money-saving tips/ Click NO if you prefer losing money through your current system." Most people will click YES because of course, they want to learn the free money saving tips, especially when the alternative is losing money. By performing that first action, they have demonstrated loyalty by aligning themselves to your brand, and they will demonstrate consistency by being receptive to the tips you provide.

Another way to make the consistency principle work for you is to encourage loyal customers to strengthen their commitment by publicly declaring their loyalty. For example, set up a Facebook competition where viewers must "like" the post, share it, and tag three friends; or an Instagram competition where they can share a photograph of themselves enjoying your product.

Australia jewelry retailer, Michael Hill Jewelers has an Instagram hashtag #mymichaelhill, where customers can announce their engagement with a photograph of them posing with their new engagement ring – purchased from Michael Hill Jewelers, of course. This Instagram account has the benefit of showcasing the store's range of engagement rings, displayed on the hands of real people rather than models, as well as creating a link of loyalty between customer and retailer beyond the original transaction.

Framing Effect

People will trust your claims more readily if you use numbers to give a context to the claim. For example, *90% of women reported visible improvement after using the product daily for two weeks.* This shows that you have tested the product and monitored results. Naturally, you must use the framing to present positive results or the claim will turn customers away from your product.

Loss Aversion

Just as people can build brand loyalty, they will also be distrustful of new brands and products, particularly if they are expected to pay for the product. You can counteract the loss aversion by offering a money back guarantee or a free trial, so the customer feels more confident about paying for your product.

The way you word your pricing can make a great deal of difference to your customer's response. For example, if you are providing a service and want to encourage people to book by a certain time, offer an early bird discount rather than setting a late fee. People will see the discounted price as lower than the regular price, so they will be keen to book early and catch a bargain; but if they miss the discount, they will be philosophical about paying the regular price. However, if you set a late fee for people who want to book after the deadline, they will be less willing to pay "extra."

Acquiescence Effect

There are three scenarios where people are more likely to acquiesce to our requests, so if you can establish these scenarios with your target customer, you will have more success in closing a sale.

The first acquiescence scenario is when you present yourself as having superior knowledge on the relevant topic. Customers are more likely to acquiesce to your sales technique if you present yourself successfully as an expert in your particular field. Consider for yourself whether you would prefer to take financial advice from a finance expert or from someone who was delegated to sell a financial product.

The second acquiescence scenario is when you ask your customer for assistance, such as asking them to write a review or share a link on social media.

The third acquiescence scenario is when it is easier to agree than to answer a question more fully. This is similar to the consistency strategy above, where you ask people to answer Yes or No to a question, when the Yes response is clearly phrased to be the "correct" response, so answering "No" would require more effort to rationalize and explain the thought process behind the response.

In Summary

We are in a new era of marketing where we can direct our advertising straight to the target audience.

Your brand is defined by a *visually compelling* image coupled with an *engaging narrative* tailored to your target audience.

Your *marketing role* is to identify the target customer and create a marketing strategy based on the four points – *product, pricing, positioning and placement.*

Create a *customer avatar* as a character profile of your ideal customer, so you can direct all your messages to this one "person."

Create a *sense of need* around your product, based on your target customer's worldview and ideal lifestyle.

Create an *authentic story* that promotes the values you uphold, which are also the same values as your target customer. Use emotion to ensure the message resonates with your target customer. Your story should also inspire a sense of familiarity and trust, making a promise to your target customer as well as to your company team.

When establishing platforms for your marketing message, make sure your strategies are *measurable* so you can make internal or external changes if necessary, and so you can ensure you see results for your investment of time and money.

Create a *self-sustaining* marketing strategy based on *four stages*: firstly, trigger the customer's sense of want; second, shift the customer's thinking to create a new perception where they feel a need for the product; third, encourage the customer to contact you; and finally, encourage the customer to promote your product or service to their own network. This is a cyclical strategy, designed so your business increases its customer base and gains momentum as you increase your market range of products or services.

Some marketing strategies are based on *behavioral psychology* and can help you tailor your campaigns to appeal to basic human behavioral instincts.

Of course, the most compelling test of your marketing strategies is the way they translate into profit. So, in the next chapter, we will look at how you can set financial benchmarks to monitor your progress.

Chapter 7 - Financial Parameters and Benchmarks to Measure Success

Most business owners' income potential is limited to no more than 3% of their potential market because they operate their business on a daily basis without a strategic plan. They only chase after the "buy now" buyers and completely forget about the buyers of the future. When you understand that 80% of your sales will come at the 5th to 12th touch point, you understand that 300% increases in sales are possible in your business when you understand your numbers and have a strategy that you are following in your business to grow it.

Yankees legend Yogi Berra once said: "If you don't know where you are going, you'll end up someplace else." This saying resonates with me as a business owner and entrepreneur striving for success. If you don't define success, how do you measure your achievements? If you don't know what you want to achieve with your business, you will take the wrong direction and risk losing the passion and independence that should be a central part of being your own boss.

In this chapter, we look at how you can set financial parameters, benchmarks, and a time frame to stay on track with your ultimate vision for your small business.

Developing a Strategic Plan
As we discussed earlier, a strategic plan gives you a "road map" outlining the long-term goals for your business and the

strategies you intend to apply in order to achieve those goals over the next 3-5 years. The three key questions forming the basis of a strategic plan are:

- What do we do?
- Who are we doing this for?
- How do we achieve the best results?

The strategic plan is also an opportunity to outline strategic risks and work out strategies to address these issues if they arise.

While large corporations can afford to invest a great deal of time into a strategic plan, and stick rigidly to it, a small business can find it more beneficial to keep the strategic plan more flexible. You do not want to over-invest your time and energy into researching a detailed long-term strategic plan if this takes you away from actually building your business and interacting with your customers. Secondly, your advantage over larger, corporation-scale competitors is your flexibility, and a rigid strategic plan can reduce your ability to shift direction when necessary.

It is also important that your strategic plan reflects the vision of all the key players in your small business. For example, if you are a chiropractor, your practice income is limited to the number of patients you can see per hour. I have worked as a consultant to numerous chiropractors and most of them can see a maximum of 50 to 60 patients per day. Within this business formula, the growth of your practice's income and profitability is limited to what you can earn per hour.

However, if you offer health coaching and nutritional education as part of your practice, you can now enter the global marketplace. Your practice can now help people on a global scale, while earning money 24/7. With this additional income, you could spend more time with each patient, improving the quality of your service, while increasing the revenue in your practice at the same time. Create a strategic plan that reflects your vision for your company, rather than imitating a strategic plan designed for a major corporation. Stay true to your own aspirations for your business and keep it flexible so you can adapt when necessary.

The Arm's Length Principle

Before we look at budgeting and financials for your business, I want to emphasize the importance of keeping your business and personal money separate or at arm's length. Not only is this basic common sense from a budgeting point of view, it also protects you from penetrating the liability veil of your LLC or Corporation.

The Arm's Length Principle (ALP) is the principle of keeping different parties within a transaction at "arm's length" on an equal footing. In the case of your small business, the "different parties" involved are you as an individual and the business itself. When you keep your personal finances separate from business finances, you can protect your personal assets from any business liabilities.

Even as a business owner, you are essentially an employee of the business, entitled to earn a salary. The money you earn becomes part of your personal assets rather than business profit, and this is an important differentiation to make if someone is demanding excessive payment from your business. Establishing distinctly separate financial records for your personal money and your business funds is the foundation of asset protection. It is generally recommended that you place at least some of your personal assets into a trust, as this can help to shield your assets from legal claims.

You might be tempted to invest your personal assets into your business, in order to ensure growth and financial security. However, this only puts your personal financial security at risk. If a creditor is seeking funds from your business, you could potentially lose your home and all your savings, making it more difficult for you to protect and restore your business while maintaining your income. While you keep your business funds and personal funds at arm's length, they remain equal partners while you retain personal security.

Your Capital Budget and Operating Budget

As a small business owner, you need a well-planned budget to ensure you can achieve your desired business income. This fundamentally comes down to setting a capital budget and an operational budget to set a plan for your finances. You will manage the financial side of your business more smoothly if you understand the key similarities and differences between these two types of budget and how they work together to support your business.

Your capital budget is your budget for capital expenditures or assets such as property or equipment that should generate income and reasonably last for more than one year. You use cash in hand for capital expenditures, so essentially you are reinvesting your earnings into assets for the business. These expenses should then in turn generate more income for the business.

Your operating budget is the annual budget for your business, based on an estimate of the total value of the resources required for the business to perform profitably. Your operating budget describes the income-generating activities of your business, and includes a forecasted income statement and the operating profit margin.

Expenses covered by the operating budget include daily expenses such as wages, utilities, rent, loan repayments, and the cost of any items intended to last less than a year. Maintenance of assets is also covered by the operational budget. It is important to plan ahead and set your operational budget so you only purchase what is necessary to maintain business activities and generate income.

For example, if you need a printer for your business, the cost of the printer is listed in your capital budget, but the cost of paper, print cartridges, and any repairs and maintenance are covered by your operational budget. If you take out a loan to purchase the printer, the loan repayment becomes an operational expense.

As you can probably see, balancing the two budgets is fairly important for the smooth running of your business. If too much of your budget is going to operational costs, you won't have enough funds for the more-costly capital expenses and this in turn can compromise your overall profitability. If you spend excessively on capital items, you will increase your operational expenses through additional maintenance or insurance fees.

According to Info Tech Research Group, your percentage of all expenditures should be around 33% for capital assets and 67% for operating expenses. While it is not possible to maintain this ratio at all times, it is a good idea to set a target ratio, so you can keep the two budgets balanced.

Components of the Operating Budget
In order to create a forecasted income statement, your operating budget must include:

Sales Budget
The sales budget estimates the sales in units as well as the estimated earnings from these sales. It states how many units of your product or service you expect to sell within the given timeframe, and how much you expect to earn from these sales. Working out your sales budget is the starting point of your budgeting as you need to know how much your business can earn, before you can decide the best way to make use of the earnings to strengthen and expand the company.

Naturally it takes a great deal of research to estimate your sales and earnings in advance, yet it is important to have a clear realistic understanding of your earning capacity if you are to remain financially stable while growing your business productively.

The sales budget is based on the findings of a sales forecast, estimating what sales the business can expect over the following time period. This calculation must allow for the effect of various seasonal time periods (for example, sales might spike before Christmas and then drop to lower than usual during January) and the contribution of different platforms, such as online sales. The sales forecast must also allow for the effect of factors such as economic changes, pricing policies, and competition.

As any of these factors can change at any time, it is good practice to regularly review your sales budget to ensure the forecast is compatible with current conditions. Once you have thoroughly researched your sales forecast, you can use these figures to set a realistic sales budget, which will set the framework for your other budgets.

Production Budget

Once your sales budget has established how many units your business can sell in a given time period, your production budget must outline how many units of the product must be produced to meet sales needs and maintain an appropriate inventory. The production budget is divided into three sections:

The **direct materials purchases budget** covers the raw material needed for the production process, calculating the cost and amount required of each type of raw material.

The **direct labor budget** covers the budgeted hours required to achieve the necessary output.

The **overhead budget** includes all other production expenses not classified as raw material or direct labor.

Ending Finished Goods Inventory Budget
This is where you calculate the value of each product, based on the cost of direct materials, direct labor, and overhead budget.

Cost of Goods Sold Budget
This is the accumulated total of all the costs that went towards creating the product and services once the product has been sold. The cost of goods sold is then deducted from the revenue to find the gross margin of the business.

Selling, General, and Administrative (SG & A) Expenses Budget
The cost of actually selling the products and services also needs to be budgeted. These costs include all the operating costs not included in the cost of goods sold. It is important to monitor these expenses as they will have a strong effect on whether you break even or make a profit. SG & A expenses include: accounting and legal expenses; corporate expenses; facility expenses; and sales and marketing expenses. They do not generally include research and development expenses or financing costs.

Budgeted Income Statement
These eight budgets fit together to incorporate the budgeted or forecasted income statement, which will reveal your company's operating income.

Cost Management Strategy
Once you start breaking down all the different costs involved in producing and delivering your product or service, you

should find it easier to identify ways to reduce expenses where necessary. And you should also be able to identify ways that spending money will make the business more cost-effective over the long term. By monitoring your costs carefully and maintaining your budget, you can increase the profitability of your business.

Cost management doesn't necessarily mean cutting all your costs to the bone. You need to provide your customers with quality products or services, delivered within a timely manner, or they will go elsewhere. If you cut costs on raw materials, you may find that you have compromised on quality or quantity, so you cannot satisfy the demands of your customers. While cost cutting might boost your profits in the short term, it will undermine your long-term relationship with customers.

However, when you monitor your outgoing expenses carefully, you will be able to identify unnecessary costs or opportunities to reduce costs without compromising on quality. Just as importantly, you will have a realistic understanding of what level of profit you can expect, if you are selling quality products or services to the public at a price they are prepared to pay.

Your business incurs two different types of costs – fixed costs and variable costs. Fixed costs are incurred in the daily operation of your business, and they are fairly predictable so you can budget for them quite easily. Variable costs are less predictable as they vary based on how much you sell. These include your raw materials and product inventory, so when demand for your product rises, your variable costs will also rise as you need to spend more on materials. When you examine your costs closely, you can identify areas of over-spending where the outgoing costs are not generating an appropriate level of income. Once you identify areas of overspending, you can cut costs without undermining the smooth running of the business. In order to work out where to cut costs and where to spend, you will need to establish a cost management strategy.

Work Out Where Your Money Is Going

If you are keeping accurate and thorough records of your expenditure, you should know exactly where all your funds are being distributed. Programs like QuickBooks can create an expense report for the last year, reviewing the percentage of money going to salaries, capital expenditure, wholesale purchases and miscellaneous costs.

Review Your Margins

Look at how much it costs to create your product or service and compare this to the sales price. Can you improve your profit margin? Are you concentrating too much on low margin sales when you could be promoting those items offering higher margins? Are there any ways you can increase the margin on your products or services without compromising on quality? Create a budget for both fixed and variable costs and examine the following areas to identify any cost cutting opportunities:

- Cost of goods and services
- Printing and production
- Employee salaries, bonuses, training and other amenities
- Computer equipment
- Utilities (for example, rent and telecommunications)
- Financing

- Marketing and signage
- Office maintenance

Stick to the Budget and Review Regularly

Stay focused on what you want to achieve for your business, and stick with the basic arithmetic of spending where necessary to generate income and avoiding any money-draining activities that do not actually contribute to the business.

Common financial "drains" include excessive interest rates on bank loans, the cost of goods or services, and unnecessary perks for employees. When you monitor these issues regularly, you can make any necessary changes promptly by requesting lower interest rates from the bank; moving to cheaper premises to cut down on rent; searching for more competitive prices on goods and services; and establishing stricter protocols over what can be claimed as a business expense.

Another less obvious way to cut costs is to reconsider your business operating hours. Are you achieving value for money within those hours? Sometimes the cost of keeping staff over a certain timeframe can exceed the amount of revenue raised. For example, if your business is open for 10 hours, you will have to pay for two shifts of employees, because they cannot work for longer than 8 hours. You might find it is more productive to cut down your business hours to 8 hours, so you only have to cover one shift; alternately, you could make the second shift longer, so you have more opportunity to cover the cost of wages through higher productivity.

The secret to effective cost management is to be proactive and continuously monitor your capital and operational budget to ensure you are achieving the best margins while providing your customers with an efficient and high-quality service.

The Profit Question

Of course, one of your key goals for your business is to ensure it starts generating a profit. You need those profits for your own salary, as well as funds to reinvest into the business so it becomes even more profitable. However, most businesses do take some time to grow and become profitable. Online businesses generally become profitable faster than physical stores, because they have fewer operating expenses. It is a good idea to allow yourself a full "test" year before you start expecting to see any profits, which is another good reason to monitor your outgoing expenses like a hawk!

Realistically, it will take between 18 to 24 months for your small business to start making a profit. This is partly due to the initial expenses of setting up your business, combined with the challenge of building up a stable customer base. Businesses that do not survive the first year are generally those that have over-capitalized and counted on an almost immediate return on their investment of time and money.

According to the US Bureau of Labor, 75% of new businesses survive the first year, 69% survive the first two years, and 50% survive for five years. Keeping that 5-year mark in mind, you can plan to be in the "winning" 50% through conservative budgeting, reinvesting in your own business, and maintaining your productivity.

So how can you budget in order to stay in business for a full year without profit? First, we need to define profitability. Technically, your business becomes profitable when your revenue exceeds your expenses. However, if you are only making just enough profit to maintain the business and allow yourself some living expenses, you are caught on a plateau of having to work very hard for a subsistence salary. Your goal is to achieve corporate profitability, which means you still have capital remaining, once you have paid all your business-related expenses and salaries.

Once your business has achieved corporate profitability, you have additional funds to reinvest into the business, making it more productive and profitable. When you are first starting out, investors will only be happy to support your business if you can demonstrate through a business plan and pro forma income statement that you can eventually achieve corporate profitability.

A pro forma income statement has four sections:
- sales projections, which are an estimate of how many sales your business will do each month based on your market research;
- a Cost of Goods Sold budget report;
- an outline of your operating expenses; and
- your gross profit estimate

When you estimate how much income you should generate through your projected sales, and then subtract your expenses, you can calculate your gross profit. If you make a monthly report of all these figures – deducting your expenses from the total revenue from actual sales, you will be able to see when your business starts to break even and then makes a profit.

Sales Forecasting

Many of my clients are stumped by this one. How can you forecast how many sales you will make in the future? This is actually a deceptively simple calculation, using a tool provided by the Sales Lead Management Association.

The key is to figure out how many sales you *need* to make in order to create the desired amount of revenue; alternately, calculate how many sales you *can* make, based on the amount of goods or services you can physically provide to potential customers. Previously, I mentioned my work with chiropractors who were limited by the number of patients they could comfortably see in an hour or a day. You can't rush patients (or any customers) through the system without giving them satisfaction and there is a limit to the number of customers you can satisfy. Of course, if customer demand exceeds your ability to supply, you can streamline and outsource to increase your ability, but for now, we are looking at how much you can comfortably supply your maximum number of customers to make maximum revenue.

Once you know how much has to be sold in revenue, you can calculate the number of leads you need to reach that figure - keeping in mind that not every lead will result in a sale.

Now you know what you need to make and what you are capable of making at the top of your game. The next step is to source the leads to make this happen. The calculator designed by the Sales Lead Management association can calculate your sales forecast or the number of enquiries with 100% follow-up that you need to make the necessary revenue. To make the calculation, you need to enter your sales forecast in dollars; the average sales price; your follow up percentage and your market share percentage. The calculator has also fixed the number of buyers from any group of leads at 45% as research has indicated that 45% of any group of leads will buy from the business within a year.

If the result seems unsatisfactory, consider improving your follow up percentage. As we mentioned in an earlier chapter, many businesses squander sales opportunities by failing to follow up. It can take multiple follow-up connections to turn a lead into a sale. If you only follow up on 50% of your leads, you lose valuable sales opportunities. In Chapter 9, I will explain ways to improve your follow up percentage.

Setting Benchmarks for Your Business

Benchmarking is defined as determining what must be improved in your business and analyzing your competition to see how they achieve their performance levels with the goal of improving your own performance. So how do you set benchmarks for your business?

Start by identifying your key business drivers – the factors, such as resources, conditions, or processes that drive your business and are essential for its growth and success. Each business has its own key business drivers, but some examples include sales leads, operational efficiency, customer service, and environmental impact.

You can identify your key business drivers by asking four simple questions:

- *Does this factor directly affect the performance of my business?*
- *Is it measurable?*
- *Can it be compared to a standard?*
- *Can it be acted upon to improve performance?*

If the answer is "Yes" to all four questions, you have identified a key business driver for your company.

Next you must find another business to set a benchmark. This could be a business with the same target customer, a business of a similar size to yours, or a business with similar objectives. The business you choose must excel – or at least do better than you – at the particular key business driver you intend to improve.

Look at the competitor's strategic objectives and the efficiency of their processes. Can you learn from their methods and find ways to improve your own system? Do they use technology more efficiently?

Compare your costs to industry norms to see if you can improve the cost-effectiveness of your results. Also look at how your gross profit margin and net profit margin compares to others in the industry to examine the efficiency of your production processes and earning capacity. If you are reaping a lower profit margin than your competitors, you can look at ways to streamline your business and lower costs.

The Benefit of 30-Day Cycles

When you break your operational plan into 30-day cycles, you can focus on what is important within each cycle as your business develops and grows. At the same time, you can identify any weaknesses or issues and find a solution.

30-Day Plan

In the first cycle, you can concentrate on establishing your business and setting your best practices into motion.

- Establish a strong organizational structure and create strong communication channels with your business team, ensuring everybody clearly understands their role and contribution to the business.
- Identify the target customer and define the customer expectations for your company.
- Identify the "cash cow" products or services offered by your company.
- Define your Best Practices.
- Look for opportunities to prioritize and streamline your production, development, administration, and in-house communication.
- Focus on daily activities that will generate sales.

60-Day Plan

In the second cycle, you can consolidate new business relationships with both customers and your business team, and review your business processes to see if you can streamline them.

- Build collaborative relationships with your business team. Focus on team leadership and strong communication.

- Establish strong customer relationships and a system for following leads.
- Solicit feedback from your business team and customers.
- Review production strategy to see if it can be streamlined.
- Review budget to see if it can be streamlined.
- Streamline business functions and reporting methods.
- Review marketing and promotional strategies.

90-Day plan

In the third cycle, you can identify new opportunities while reviewing and assessing how you are meeting your initial business goals.

- Identify current and prospective customers.
- Identify strategies for streamlining production, budget, or customer service.
- Establish performance metrics for future evaluations.
- Evaluate marketing strategies.

In Summary

In order to succeed in business, you need to create a **definition of success**, and from there you can measure your achievements. You need to know what you want to achieve with your business, in order to reach your desired goal. In this chapter, we looked at ways to set financial parameters, benchmarks, and timeframes to achieve your ultimate vision for your business.

A **strategic plan** creates a road map for your business, outlining long-term goals and the strategies you intend to apply to achieve those goals over the next 3 to 5 years. The strategic plan

is based on the response to three key questions:
- What do we do?
- Who are we doing this for?
- How do we achieve the best results?

As a small business, you want to ensure that you do not overinvest your time and energy into researching a strategic plan, as you will find it more beneficial to keep the plan simple and flexible.

When you structure your finances, be sure to follow the **Arm's Length Principle** and separate your personal finances from your business accounts. This will help to protect your personal assets if the business runs into financial trouble and vice-versa.

A well-planned budget for a small business is comprised of a capital budget and an operational budget. The **capital budget** covers the cost of capital expenditures or assets such as property or equipment that should generate income and reasonably last more than one year. The **operating budget** covers expenses such as wages, utilities, rent, maintenance of capital items, loan repayments, and the cost of any items intended to last less than one year. These two budgets should ideally be balanced at 33% for capital assets and 67% for operating expenses.

The operating budget must include the following components in order to create a forecasted income statement:
Sales Budget – estimates the sales in units and the estimated earnings from these sales, how many units you intend to sell within the given timeframe, and how much you expect to earn

from these sales. This budget is based on the findings of the sales forecast.

Production Budget – outlines how many units of the product are needed to meet sales demand and maintain the inventory. This budget is divided into three sections: direct materials purchases budget, covering the cost of raw materials; direct labor budget; overhead budget, for expenses not classified as raw material or direct labor.

Ending Finished Goods Inventory Budget – calculates the value of each product, based on costs of materials, labor and overhead.

Cost of Goods Sold Budget – accumulated total of all the costs involved in creating the product or service. This is deducted from the revenue to establish the gross margin of the business. Selling, General, and Administrative (SG&A) Expenses Budget – covers the cost of actually selling products and services, including expenses for accounting, legal, corporate, facility, and marketing.

Your **cost management strategy** involves your management of fixed costs and variable costs in order to provide prompt and high quality goods or services to your customers. Fixed costs are incurred in daily business operation, and are fairly predictable, while variable costs include raw materials and product inventory.

Your cost management strategy involves keeping strict records of outgoing expenditures, reviewing margins, and reviewing budget to identify any financial drains. Allow for between 18 to 24 months before your small business makes a profit.

Sales forecasting involves calculating how many sales you need to make to achieve the desired revenue. This will also show you what percentage of leads you need to follow up on to achieve this amount.

Benchmarking is a strategy for determining what may be improved in your business, by analyzing how your competition achieve their performance levels. Start by identifying your key business drivers then find another business or research industry norms to set a benchmark.

Break your operational plan into **30 day cycles,** so you can focus on what is important within each cycle, while identifying and solving any issues or weaknesses.

As your business grows and becomes more complex, you will find it easier to keep a handle on expenses if you systemize every aspect of your activities. We will discuss business systems and how they improve efficiency in the next chapter.

Chapter 8 - Systemizing Your Business

I have often encountered small business owners who have created unnecessary obstacles for themselves by taking ownership of too many "little" jobs, so they don't have the time or creative energy to tackle the "big" jobs. Visualize your business as a stone bridge that must be built across a river. As the manager, you must concentrate on working out the best design and structure for the bridge. Gather the experts to make it a reality, provide the funds to pay for materials and labor, and then promote the new bridge as a great place to cross the river. If you put your energy into gathering the stones for the bridge, those important and unique decisions are neglected, and the stones won't necessarily be gathered any faster.

As the business owner, you must dedicate your insight and energy towards the decisions nobody else can make. Delegate the stone-gathering to your team. This approach ensures that all the major decisions are in line with your business philosophy and you can set the deadlines and priorities necessary to make the "bridge" a reality. It is also economically sound, as you should be creating a higher rate of revenue per hour than the other members of your team. While you are focused on the smaller, low-rate tasks, you are failing to draw in the high revenue that other members of your team cannot achieve.

You can balance your business tasks by systemizing your business and setting clear responsibilities for all your team members. This way, all the tedious yet necessary tasks are completed in a timely efficient manner and the larger long-term responsibilities are given the right level of expert attention. By balancing all responsibilities within the system, your business becomes more productive and profitable.

The Benefits of Systemization

A system is any procedure or policy that is designed to consistently achieve the same result, even with a different operator in charge. With a series of systems in place, you can ensure that the underlying processes of your business proceed smoothly and efficiently, so products are made, customers receive responsive service, safety procedures are observed, invoices are sent, and bills are paid.

Each system involves a simple step-by-step procedure designed to achieve the desired result. The person running the system can confidently take ownership of the task at hand, and if necessary, another person can take over and achieve the same outcome.

By systemizing your business, you make it more self-sustaining. You don't need to stay back at night stamping envelopes to send the invoices, and you don't need to deprive yourself of vacations in order to monitor the production line. Even if you are not on the spot, the system is operating, and the business will keep providing goods and services while generating revenue.

You are managing your own time more efficiently which means you are also investing the cost of employee salaries and contractor fees more wisely, because your employees and contractors will generate more revenue when working within a streamlined system.

A systemized business is also a more enticing investment for potential buyers when you are ready to sell up and retire. You are selling a proven streamlined and profitable business, that they can tailor to their business perspective while remaining confident that the business administration is self-sufficient. Your business will sell for up to 300% of its value because you have a franchise type system created and documented in your business.

Establishing a System

Before you establish a system, look at how you manage the task right now. What is your current procedure for sending an invoice to a client? Are there ways of streamlining the process? Once the invoice is sent, how do you keep track of whether it has been paid?

Look at ways of streamlining the process so you can send invoices more efficiently, with an effective follow-up procedure in place.

Alternately, ask your team to keep a log of all the different tasks they perform in a week, making a note of how long it takes each person to complete each task. This will help you define employee roles and identify the strengths of each team member, so you can delegate each task to the best person for the job. You might also identify some convoluted system already in place, leading you to figure out a faster and more effective way to move tasks through to completion.

There will be countless systems, large and small, within your business, so it helps to identify all the tasks and then work through each task individually, identifying the most efficient and accurate way to complete this step in the overall procedure.

So, what is your system for establishing a system?

First, create a list of simple and comprehensible step-by-step instructions explaining in a linear process how to complete the relevant task. Review the instructions with employees who generally complete the task to confirm that you haven't neglected an essential step, and that you haven't made the procedure too difficult to follow. Then ask someone else to follow the instructions so you can see if they make sense to someone who doesn't usually work at this task.

Next, test the system over a prescribed period (such as a week or a month) to ensure that it works seamlessly with minimal supervision or input. Gather feedback to confirm whether it meets the expectations of customers, suppliers and employees. If there are any issues, amend the system to correct the flaws and start again with another testing period. It is a good idea to schedule regular evaluations of your system to ensure it still achieves its required goal, even as your business grows and changes.

The third step is to train employees in the new system and pay attention to their feedback. Finally, once the system is in place, delegate the various tasks to different people within your business. Your ultimate goal as business owner is to delegate these repetitive and essential tasks to others, so you can concentrate on the "bigger picture."

Once you are satisfied that the system is running seamlessly and there are plenty of back up employees capable of taking control if necessary, then your system is in place.

Types of Systems for Your Small Business

There is still a place for manual systems and procedures in the workplace, such as a chain of approval for large expenses, instruction manuals, or an established protocol for business meetings to ensure they are efficient and effective. In today's world, there are also many electronic options to help your business run smoothly, with the added benefit of keeping a clear record of projects and expenditures.

The right software system can streamline your business, storing a comprehensive range of key information and improving the functionality of all your operations. Groupware software is a good option for a business that relies on collaboration and strong teamwork between employees, as it facilitates electronic communication such as voice files and can include project management tools.

There are six general areas of your business that can benefit from systemization.

Administration

Administrative tasks are ideal for systemization as they are essential "background" tasks which are generally repetitive, yet they also tend to have a strong impact on the customer's perception of your business. If your accountant is sick, can someone else send out the invoices? Does your new receptionist know how to answer the phone correctly and set up conference calls for meetings? Do the members of your call center have a clear understanding of your company policies, so they can pass on the correct information to your customers?

Without a series of clearly outlined systems, your business could become disorganized, messy, and vulnerable to security breaches. Is your meeting room consistently tidy and organized when you open the door for clients? How do you manage all the paper that your business will inevitably generate? What should be thrown away as waste paper and what should be filed? Who is responsible for unlocking the office door every morning and locking up each night? How many people know the code to the burglar alarm and who has access to the petty cash?

With clear procedures in place for every aspect of administration, you will be able to concentrate on the business at hand without being distracted by avoidable complications and obstacles.

Accounting

Accounting, of course, is based purely on mathematics and you need accurate records in order to monitor the all-important difference between your outgoing expenditures and your incoming payments. Accounting software can record and measure your sales, costs and profits, as well as generate invoices automatically, so you can monitor the financial side of your business as efficiently and accurately as possible. These financial software systems will streamline your procedures, from purchasing costs to client invoices and tax payments. Keep in mind that the number one security threat to any business is actually from internal users. So, choose an accounting system that identifies individual user activity and makes sure all your employees know they are accountable for their individual actions.

Communication

Your communication system is essential to support your interaction with your employees as well as with your customers. Like administrative tasks, your communication tasks tend to be repetitive, yet in this case it is also important to address the individual aspects of each subject of communication.

Set up a standard structure and format for every type of letter, newsletter, internal memo, and minutes of meetings. For example, if you have a standard form letter to respond to customer complaints, you can simply add some additional details to address the individual concerns so the letter is completed quickly and remains courteous and professional. For any employees who are repeatedly calling customers or answering calls, give them a comprehensive outline of your policies, along with a phone call script to follow, so they gather all the essential information and give the most appropriate response to each caller.

Customer relations is an important element of your communication procedures, so you should have systematic procedures in place to manage the sales process and general customer liaison. It is particularly important to have a strong procedure in place to deal with complaints, so the problem can be contained and the customer will be satisfied that the issue has been resolved.

Invest in a phone system that supports your in-house communication as well as with customers. When looking for a phone system, ask yourself if you will need multimedia connectivity, video conferencing, or call center applications so you can establish the right system for your business needs.

Employees
From the first interview, you need systems and protocols in place to ensure you hire and retain the best employees for each position, and that they understand their rights and responsibilities.

As part of your responsibility to your employees, you need to establish suitable training and personal development programs and regular reviews. You must also provide job descriptions and role profiles, so each team member understands their role within the system and what they are expected to achieve.

Time and money are your two most valuable commodities, and just as you need to understand and monitor expenditures, you must also track how you and your employees spend their time. Time management systems improve your productivity and expand your resources. You can also calculate how much time realistically goes into each task, so you know how much to charge for a project and you can identify the most efficient team members for each task.

Data Management
Your data management systems keep your office organized

and help you differentiate between important pieces of paper and rubbish. The data backup system is a key element of data management as you need to protect your intellectual property and your customer records in case anything happens to your computer software.

Marketing

Strong and measurable marketing systems are essential to ensure you are generating new leads and creating effective promotions. You must also have a system in place to follow up on leads regularly. Marketing systems can include enquiries management, customer retention programs, referral programs, direct mail systems, sales procedures, and lead management.

Today, there are two strands of marketing – online and offline marketing, also known as digital and traditional marketing. While you use completely different strategies for each form of marketing, it is important to ensure that the online and offline campaigns complement each other. Many small businesses take an inconsistent approach, running marketing campaigns with different styles and agendas, leading to brand confusion. Alternately, they choose to work with either traditional or digital, not both, losing a significant portion of their target audience.

In my experience, working with small business owners, I find the most common marketing problem is a poorly synchronized marketing campaign. So, we will look more closely at how to systemize your marketing strategy to ensure the online and offline marketing campaigns for your business are working in alignment.

Systemizing Online and Offline Marketing

Offline marketing is another term for traditional marketing – magazine advertisements, television commercials, and billboards, all designed to increase general exposure and recognition of your brand. Online or digital marketing refers to any strategy that attracts customers to your online profile, through emails, web content, or social media.

Digital marketing has the advantage of directly targeting your ideal customer and it is also directly measurable, unlike traditional marketing which is more expensive and cannot directly prove its results. However, traditional marketing is more appealing to those who prefer a traditional customer experience, such as face to face service and purchasing items in person rather than online. So, when you combine the two, you have a formidable marketing formula that will attract the full spectrum of your target audience.

Complementary Promotion

The key to synchronizing your two marketing campaigns is to make them promote each other. Your magazine advertisement can include an online call-to-action, such as giving your target audience an incentive to join your Facebook page, download your free eBook, or sign up for your newsletter. Your online campaign can draw people into your store, through discounts and special offers, and a social media campaign can invite people to a special event.

One of the most notable combined online/offline campaigns was launched by a company called Warby Parker, an American brand of prescription glasses and sunglasses. Warby Parker devised a marketing scheme to encourage people to purchase prescription glasses and sunglasses online. The challenge was that people prefer to try on the glasses to see that the frames are comfortable and flattering, Warby Parker established a "Home-Try-On program" allowing customers to select five frames from the website, which are then delivered to their home free of charge. The customer has five days to try the frames before making their selection. Warby Parker also provides an online tool where customers can upload a photo so they can "try on" different pairs of glasses virtually.

Live chat is another online tool that companies can use to give them the edge in the offline world. Businesses that rely on real time meetings to discuss or close a deal can expand their scope by providing life chat on their website, so visitors can ask questions and request files or other information. The real estate industry in particular benefits from the opportunity to forge a personal bond online with potential buyers who might physically be too far away for a real-world meeting.

Systematic Style

As we've mentioned previously, the key to a recognizable brand image is consistency and simplicity. Your marketing campaign should be founded on a clear style guide so the company's online and offline campaigns use the same colors, phrasing, and "voice." You can include a list of approved stock phrases and images to maintain consistency. Your style guide should also outline a protocol for responding to any online questions or complaints, to ensure that these responses remain courteous and accurate.

Outsourcing

Once you have established these systematic tasks, you need people to run each system. One of the benefits of a good system, as mentioned above, is that anyone with the relevant background knowledge, should be able to step in and run the system.

This increases your "bus number," making your business less dependent on one or two people to run smoothly. The term "bus number" refers to the number of individuals who would have to be "hit by a bus" or suffer some kind of catastrophe before your business would suffer. If only one person knows the password to your computer system, then you have a bus number of one – if that person is hit by a bus and unable to show up at work or even communicate on the phone, then your business is inoperable. While you only need a limited bus number of individuals with access to sensitive information, your goal with outsourcing is to create an indefinite bus number on the simple but essential tasks relating to the running of your business.

As a consultant, I have met many small business owners who claim they "can't afford" to outsource tasks to contractors, arguing that they don't want to pay someone to do the work they can complete themselves for free. However, when you insist on handling every aspect of the business yourself, you limit your potential for growth. I have found that outsourcing can increase business productivity by 300% simply by expanding the number of hours your business is operational, while enabling senior team members to concentrate on more lucrative and specialized tasks.

The Benefits of Outsourcing

Outsourcing, also known as Business Process Outsourcing, is the process of hiring another individual or company to take charge of specific business tasks for your company. When you use outsourcing as part of your business plan from the very beginning, you establish a flexible infrastructure that can grow alongside your business, benefiting from expert attention in every area and keeping your business cost effective. When every team member is working to the best of their ability without being distracted by tasks outside their skillset, your business automatically becomes more efficient, streamlined and productive.

Deciding When to Outsource

Tasks for outsourcing can be divided into three basic categories – basic administrative tasks, specialist tasks, and what I call obstacle tasks.

Basic administrative tasks are the simple repetitive tasks that can become tedious but need to be done. Examples include responding to emails, sending items to customers, or even basic household tasks. These are the "little" jobs that can overwhelm you and distract you from the real jobs that must be done.

Specialist tasks are those jobs which are performed with greater efficiency and expertise by a specialist in the field. You might feel that you can do these jobs yourself, but if you don't have the enthusiasm or the background experience, you won't necessarily achieve the most professional results – and while you are struggling to complete the self-appointed task, you are neglecting the jobs that are within your expertise. Examples include, blog writing, accounting, research, and information technology.

The "obstacle" tasks are those elements of your job that you find most difficult or tedious, so you slow your own progress by procrastinating or spending too much time trying to complete them to a professional standard. While you might think it unprofessional to admit you are struggling, it is actually more professional to ensure the job is done enthusiastically and efficiently.

Keeping Outsourcing Cost-effective
If you are concerned about the cost of building up a business team of experts before your business is profitable, consider hiring contractors or freelancers. This way, you can pay an hourly rate for their expertise when and if you need it, plus you have the option of building a strong relationship with contractors who are a good fit with your team.

The Internet allows you to invite contractors from anywhere over the world to join your team, giving you the freedom to turn your local business into a global concern, staying productive around the clock. However, when you are hiring contractors online, stay vigilant to ensure you are not exploiting individuals from Third World countries who may not be paid fairly for their work. The most common sites that I hire contractors from are Upwork.com and Fiverr.com.

Retaining Control Over Your Business

While you may be concerned that outsourcing could potentially undermine your control over your business, the opposite is actually true. If you start outsourcing from the beginning while your business is small, you create a small yet manageable infrastructure that you can easily oversee. This gives you the opportunity to create a strong foundation of communication and consistent protocol that will help keep the business on track as it grows. When this infrastructure is made up of contractors and freelancers, it remains quite flexible so you can expand or reduce your business when necessary.

As you can see, systemizing your business can turn your small local company into a global organization, increasing your business hours from 8 hours each weekday to 24 hours a day, 7 days a week, and creating a simple yet powerful infrastructure that capitalizes on the strengths and passions of each team player. And you can do all this on a relatively small budget, building and expanding as you go, so the strength and security of your business keeps pace with its growth. If you would like to learn more about outsourcing, we have several programs available to help you increase your sales, profitability, leadership skills, and productivity. If you would like to know more and get updates on coming events, please visit: http://peakprofitacademy.com.

In Summary

Systemizing your business is the first step towards creating a self-sufficient and cost-effective enterprise, which will continue making revenue even when you are not around to supervise. From here, your business becomes an attractive

investment opportunity which you can sell when you are ready to retire. When you outsource contractors to run the systems within your business, you can **increase your productivity by 300%,** improving efficiency and increasing revenue at a corresponding rate.

A **system** is any procedure or policy designed to consistently achieve the same result, even with a different operator in charge. Each system involves a simple step-by-step procedure designed to achieve the desired result. The person in charge of the system, can take ownership, and another person can take over and achieve the same outcome.

With a series of systems in place, you can be confident that the underlying processes of your business proceed smoothly and efficiently, maintaining production, safety, profit, and customer satisfaction.

Systemizing your business makes it more self-sustaining and ensures you manage your own time more efficiently. The business will generate more revenue within a streamlined system.

Establish a system by creating a list of simple step-by-step instructions to explain a linear process for completing a task. Review the instructions with employees or contractors who generally complete the task so they can confirm you haven't missed a step, and that it is not too difficult to follow. Ask someone else to follow the instructions to confirm that they make sense and achieve the correct purpose. Next test the system over a prescribed period, gathering feedback to confirm whether it meets expectations of customers, suppliers and employees. The final step is to train employees in the system, and pay attention to their feedback. Schedule regular evaluations as your business expands, to ensure each system still achieves the required goal.

Systems can be established in the following areas: administration; accounting; communication; employees; data management; and marketing. One particularly important marketing system is the synchronization of your online and offline marketing campaigns to ensure they complement each other.

Outsourcing provides the team members to run the systems you have established. Benefits of outsourcing include increasing the "**bus number**" of individuals capable of running essential systems and protocols; establishing a flexible infrastructure that can grow alongside your business; and expanding your productivity from local office hours to 24 hours, 7 days a week; making the business more efficient, streamlined, and productive.

Tasks for **outsourcing** can be divided into three categories: administrative, specialist, and obstacle tasks. You can keep outsourcing cost effective and flexibility by hiring contractors or freelancers from around the globe.

Having covered marketing, financials, and the systems which keep these business elements efficient and effective, we will take a closer look at the system which can revolutionize your marketing strategy.

Chapter 9 - Marketing and Sales Automation

Marketing automation is software that literally automates your marketing strategy so you can enhance and expand all the best qualities of a strong marketing campaign. With automation your business can be more engaging, more recognizable, and more trustworthy in the eyes of customers and prospects. So, how does marketing automation achieve this?

Nurture Relationships

The purpose of marketing automation is to nurture relationships with leads that aren't ready to buy. On average, only 20% of leads are sales-ready when they first come in. So, you need a disciplined process – known as lead nurturing – to develop qualified leads until they are sales-ready. When it is done well, nurturing can result in 50% more sales leads at 33% lower cost per lead.

Retain and Extend Customer Relationships

The marketer's job is far from finished once someone becomes a customer. For most industries, the real value comes from retaining and deepening the customer relationship over time. This includes selling more of the same product to the customer (up-sell), selling additional products to the customer (cross-sell), as well as customer loyalty and retention. Note that relationship marketing means more than sending a monthly newsletter. You need multiple tracks for each buyer persona and buying stage that "listen" to how the customer behaves, and adjusts accordingly – just like a real-world relationship.

Beyond the time-saving and efficiency benefits of automation, marketing automation enables modern business processes that are essential to any modern marketing department. For B2B companies, this includes lead nurturing, lead scoring, and lead lifecycle management. For B2C companies, it includes cross-sell, up-sell, and retention. And for all companies, it includes marketing ROI analytics.

Build Alignment with Sales
Many of the so-called "leads" you generate are not true potential buyers for your products. You need "demographic lead scoring" to find the customers that fit your target profile. You also need "behavioral lead scoring" to find the hot ones displaying buying behaviors that indicate that they are ready to engage with you and make a purchase. And, once you've identified a lead as "hot," you want to make sure your Sales team follows up quickly – and in a relevant manner, so you need integration with CRM and automation of processes like sales alerting, lead recycling, and service level agreements (SLA).

According to the Marketo Benchmark on Revenue Performance, companies that implement this kind of lead scoring enjoy 28% better sales productivity and 33% higher revenue growth than companies without lead scoring. Learn more by downloading Marketo's *Definitive Guide to Lead Scoring* https://www.marketo.com/definitive-guides/lead-scoring/.

Prove and Improve – Marketing ROI
Marketing automation goes beyond process automation to help marketing executives get much-needed insight into which

marketing programs are working and which are not effective. It gives CMOs the metrics they need to speak confidently to the C-suite about Marketing's revenue impact.

With the Profit Faucet™ systems implemented in your business, you can turn cash flow on and off in your business at will. Marketing and sales automation is one of the key components of The Profit Faucet™.

Did you ever wonder how some businesses are achieving triple digit increases in sales? Let me explain some key facts about sales cycles, so you understand how a 300%+ increase in sales is possible. We know that 80% of the sales in your business will come at the 5th to 12th touch point[1] with a prospect. Most business owners don't do more than two or three touch points with a prospect before they move on to the next opportunity.

There simply aren't enough hours in the day to hit five or more touch points with a prospect. Your business is stuck, only capable of reaching a maximum of 3% of your potential market due to the lack of follow up systems in your business. Imagine being able to follow up on 100% of all your potential leads and pulling in a steady stream of new leads on autopilot to keep your pipeline full of potential buyers. You have the automation systems in place to greet them at every stage of the buyer's journey. When they are ready to buy, there you are to greet them with a friendly "How would you like to pay?"

The buyer's journey is a three-step process. Step 1 is the awareness stage, when they become aware they have a problem they need to solve. Step 2 is the consideration or research stage, where they must research a potential solution to their problem. Step 3 is the decision stage, where they decide upon the solution and settle on the seller who can provide the solution to their problem. This is where marketing automation saves your business.

Remember the B.E.E.P. process we talked about earlier in the book? Build an audience. Engage the audience, by gaining and keeping their attention through valuable content. Educate the prospect by building a relationship with them so they know, love, and trust you. Promote your solution, by making a low risk offer so the prospect will transition into a buyer. When we implement the B.E.E.P.™ process into your marketing automation strategy, you will stay one step ahead of your prospects at every stage of the Buyer's Journey.

Marketing and sales automation is a series of tools configured to operate in a defined sales process called a funnel. The funnel provides content and education to the prospects to move them through the stages of the buyer's journey. The marketing and sales process is automated through a collaboration of software, marketing, and advertising mediums to create more sales and increased profitability in your business.

Your business will experience dramatic sales increases of up to 300% in a year, simply through implementation of marketing and sales automation. You will be able to follow up with prospects at every step of the buyer's journey. They will always buy from you, because you were there, building the relationship and educating them on how to make an informed decision to solve their problem. When they are ready to implement the solution, they will buy from you.

Marketing and sales automation can never replace the need for the human interaction with your prospects or customers. Your customers buy from you because they love and trust you. They don't trust some computer or a set of tools - these tools simply facilitate your connection. You must make the most of the connection, through the follow-up and engagement with your prospects so you can move them through the buyer's journey.

Now we are ready to pull together everything we have covered in this book so you can see the big picture. Now, I will explain marketing automation as it relates to the B.E.E.P.™ Process.

B for Build an Audience - Lead Generation

As we saw earlier, collecting leads is an important first step in your marketing strategy. Approximately 27% of leads will instantly convert into customers, while the other 73% need more time to consider their options and make their decision. Some of these prospects might be extremely interested, but just not ready for your product or service; others might be comparing you to the competition as they research their options; and only a small percentage have stumbled onto your database by chance.

If you lose contact with these prospects, they might drift over to your competition who are making more of an effort to stay in the prospect's consciousness. So, it makes sense to create a system that helps you keep track of as many leads as possible and also helps you identify the stronger prospects as soon as possible.

The best way to collect leads is on a special website called a 'landing page.' A landing page is the page a visitor "lands" on when they click a link to your website. There are two types of landing pages – Click Through and Lead Generation.

The purpose of the Click Through landing page is to persuade the visitor to click through to another page, which will include an offer designed to tempt the visitor to make a purchase. The purpose of the Lead Generation page is to capture user data such as a name and email address, so this can be used to continue engaging with the prospect over time, building brand awareness and preference, increasing the likelihood of the prospect converting into a customer.

Here you can see an example of a lead capture page, https://peakprofitmedia.clickfunnels.com/optin11622799.

Lead nurturing involves maintaining contact with potential customers, while gathering information about them which can be used to evaluate their level of interest in your product or service. Armed with this information, you can send relevant targeted marketing messages to each prospect group, ensuring they are more naturally responsive to your message. Some of your customers will be more receptive to one particular message, while other customers will be drawn to a different approach.

Each prospect is on their own timeframe regarding when they intend to make their purchase. Lead nurturing through marketing automation can increase your sales leads by 50% while lowering the overall cost of acquiring the lead.

Lead scoring is a marketing technique that evaluates the demographic and behavioral characteristics as they interact with your marketing material such as web content and emails. This information helps you target your approach to the individual prospect, yet it can also be used to streamline your approach to future prospects, as you will have greater insight into their potential pattern of behavior. Demographic lead scoring will identify the customers which fit your target profile, while behavioral lead scoring tracks the behavior of leads as they transition into customers, so you can learn to recognize in advance when a lead is ready to make that transition.

Lead scoring is particularly beneficial with high value products and services, where the prospect tends to take a considerable length of time to research options before making a purchasing decision. Research from the Marketo Benchmark on Revenue Performance has found that companies that do lead scoring through marketing automation have 28% higher sales productivity than other companies, and 33% higher revenue growth.

Lead scoring software evaluates the prospect data to determine their *interest* and their *fit* with the product. You can gather this information by sending out an email questionnaire or quiz and evaluating the responses, or you can evaluate their online behavior.

You can "score" their online behavior with a simple point system based on their responses to your marketing calls to action. For example, the prospect "wins" five points if they open the marketing email, 10 points for downloading your free eBook, 20 points for following the prompts to request a free assessment, 30 points for becoming a paid subscriber, and 40 points for viewing the payment form. If the prospect disengages from your online calls to action, you deduct points from their lead score. Another way to "score" prospects is to ask direct questions about their immediate interest in the product or service. For example, one particularly valuable question is "Are you interested in buying within the next 0-3 months, 3-6 months, 6-12 months..." with higher scores for those prospects who are interested in purchasing sooner rather than later.

Once you have "scored" your customers, you can segment your lists based on their score and create custom campaigns to meet them at where they are in the buyer's journey based on their lead score. You can concentrate on those with high scores as the most likely to be ready to purchase. As your email marketing, ringless voicemail, and text messaging campaign is aligned with your marketing automation, any increase in score will trigger a targeted email, ringless voicemail, or text message to the prospect.

Research has shown that prospects who receive an email, ringless voicemail, or text message from a business within 5 minutes of their own action are far more likely to follow through with a purchase than a prospect who receives an email within 30 minutes. Just 25 minutes in response time can be the difference between a sale or no sale. Yet, you cannot maintain this response time manually.

At the same time, you can continue monitoring those prospects who had slightly lower scores as their profile may change. By differentiating your leads, you can tailor your approach according to the prospect's current level of interest.

E for Engage - Inbound Marketing

Inbound marketing is the process of building brand awareness and from there, creating brand preference so that potential customers actively seek you out when they are ready to make a purchase. As we've mentioned earlier, your brand is your public image – it must be simple, consistent, and memorable so potential customers can retain a snapshot understanding of what you provide and what values your company upholds.

When your brand is firmly established in a prospect's consciousness, they are more likely to turn to you when they have the need for your solution. From your perspective, this is a much faster, more cost-effective and efficient transition from unknown to customer, than when you seek out and nurture a prospect for an unspecified length of time.

When marketing was confined mainly to television advertisements, inbound marketing involved writing a catchy jingle that would drum the brand name and message into people's minds. If a television ad was particularly clever, funny – or even ridiculously bad or controversial – people would talk about it with their friends and family, spreading the brand consciousness further.

The disadvantage of inbound marketing is, of course, that it is not particularly tailored to your target market. You are out to attract everyone's attention, and out of those millions of people who see your advertisement on prime-time television, a small percentage will be attracted to your product and want to learn more. With traditional television advertising, the call to action was usually fairly crude – you crave that burger, or you want to take advantage of that low, low price – but when you are home in front of the television, you can't immediately act upon the impulse.

Today, unless inbound marketing is teamed with marketing automation, the result could potentially be the same. Brand awareness is only truly effective when it develops into brand preference, and you can only achieve brand preference if you target your inbound towards prospects who are more likely to desire a product or service like yours. As a small business, you can't afford to create brand awareness among millions and hope that a small percentage will follow through with a purchase; you need to target your inbound marketing to ensure that brand awareness is growing among prospects who have a genuine need for your service.

When inbound marketing is combined with marketing automation, you have the benefit of scoring potential prospects, building a relationship and providing strong calls to action, so more prospects convert into leads and customers.

E for Educate - Social and Content Marketing

Our role in our businesses is to be an educator when it comes to gaining the love and trust of our prospects and keeping our customers. We need to provide them with content that will educate and engage them in order to hold their attention and keep them as customers. The key to a successful content marketing campaigns is a content marketing strategy utilizing social marketing, email marketing, ringless voicemail, text messaging, and postcards. People crave inspiring quality content that teaches them how to solve their problems. Sharing your stories, sharing good content and tips with your target audience builds their trust so they are willing to buy from you.

Social marketing is the process of building relationships online through platforms such as Facebook, LinkedIn, Instagram, and Twitter. Content marketing is the process of distributing informative and relevant content to engage the interest of potential customers. These strategies are not intended to close with a sale – their goal is to build brand awareness and build the relationship with target audience of potential customers who are not currently considering a purchase, so brand awareness can develop into brand preference when circumstances change.

There are several common mistakes a small business owner will make in relation to social and content marketing. Firstly, they may compromise on the quality of content, so it is not original, engaging, or thought-provoking – or even grammatically correct! With so many different sources to explore online, potential customers are not going to be interested in a badly rehashed blog on a topic that had been covered thoroughly by your competitors.

Secondly, some business owners fail to address the concerns or interests of their target audience, so the content is wasted on viewers who have no interest in the product. Either of these issues separately or combined, leads to the third and most pressing issue – the time invested in the marketing campaign does not generate a profitable level of revenue. You need to ensure your content is fresh, original, and consistent, so potential customers are drawn to your brand.

Finally, it is a mistake to repeatedly share the same piece of content through every social media platform and email marketing channel. You want to share unique content over your marketing channels because you don't want to have your target audience feel like you are trying to spam them repeatedly with the same information. The content on your Facebook, Twitter, LinkedIn, Instagram, blog and email marketing must be unique to hold the attention of your target audience.

P for Promote - Make a Low Risk Offer to Invite Prospects to Work with You.

In order to move prospects through the buyer's journey, you must communicate with them in a medium that they find most comfortable for communication. Typically, the low risk offer would be to meet with a prospect over coffee, a ringless voicemail coupon that is sent to their cell phone, or a low-cost product that will help them with their particular issue. While it may not solve all their problems, it will show your prospect that you can help them. An example of a low risk offer could be an online course such as my 5x Productivity Course, where I show people how they can master outsourcing and achieve more freedom in their lives.

Here are some strategies for using marketing automation to promote the offer to the prospect:

Telephone Call
Call the prospect to make an appointment to discuss their problem and present an opportunity to work together.

Email marketing
Email marketing involves creating a simple straightforward format for emails and newsletters that are designed to resonate with various prospect and customer groups. The purpose of email marketing is to track email performance through receiver responses, whether they open the email, click on the link or follow through with a purchase. I prefer to create short emails that link to a video that is hosted on YouTube. The email discusses the content in the video so the person reading the email will click on the video while reading on their mobile device. Eighty percent of the people reading your content will read it on their mobile device, so it is important to keep this in mind when we are creating content. The prospect would click the link in the email to take advantage of the low risk offer.

Ringless Voice Mail
Ringless voice mail is a pre-recorded message delivered to your target audience's cell phone. The message is delivered directly to the voicemail of the prospect's cell phone without ringing their phone. This is an excellent way to send your prospects a short message so they will open and listen to it at their convenience. You acquire their cell phone numbers by offering them a low-cost product. You would create a 30 second message that would give the prospect a discount on your services or product.

Text Messaging

Text messaging enables you to send short friendly reminders about appointments, events, and webinars. People will respond to text messages and 30% of Americans prefer a text message over a voice call.

Evergreen Webinars

Automated Webinars are created with software or a software as a service that lets you use a recording of a presentation or even a replay of a webinar recording and to stream it live during a real-time broadcast or live webinar event. You can sell products from $300+ from a webinar.

Sales Page

A sales page is a web page or landing page which can be very beneficial for the sale of products. It is very productive for e-commerce purposes, online advertisement of a product with action button or link like "Buy Now," and "Apply Now." You can sell products from $1 to $300 from a sales page.

What to Consider When Comparing Marketing Automation Software

Before we go into the pros and cons, or the pricing comparisons, it's important to know what to look out for. It pays to do your research and investigate what you really need, and what will work for you. I have several friends who signed up for marketing automation software, only to realize one month down the line that it wasn't compatible with their CRM. Ouch.

Below are a couple of important considerations and questions to keep in mind when comparing the various software providers.

Let's start with the deal breakers. These are the first red flags you should be alert for when comparing marketing automation software providers.

Pricing

Most marketing automation tools are priced on a sliding scale with additional costs for training and add-ons. They can become ludicrously expensive very quickly if you're not careful. I'd recommend taking a 3 to 5-year perspective when weighing up your options. I prefer a fixed cost model where you can predict the cost and there are no surprises as your business grows.

Usability

Marketing automation is inherently complex. As such, usability is extremely important as it will determine how much value your team can extract from the tool. The less intuitive the software, the more you will pay for training, and the more headaches your team will endure.

Integrations with Your Existing Software

This is extremely important, yet sometimes overlooked. Some marketing automation tools only allow integration with a small number of third party apps/CRM systems.

Now, let's look at the preferences. Some of these may be deal breakers for you, but they're mostly to do with what features the software provides.

Preferences

CRM / sales capabilities

Some marketing automation tools have an built-in CRM system with lead scoring and advanced tagging capabilities. Others have no in-built CRM, as they expect you to connect the software with your existing CRM.

Email capabilities

While all marketing automation tools enable email marketing in some capacity, some are better than others. Do you need drip campaigns? Subject line A/B testing? Demographic segmentation?

Content capabilities

Do you need to create landing pages, webinars, or other forms of content to send out to your contacts? While most marketing automation tools enable this, some are easier to use and more extensive than others.

E-commerce capabilities

Do you sell products online? Some marketing automation tools, such as Infusionsoft and Ontraport, can act as your product database. These tools usually offer features like coupon codes, and affiliate programs.

Social Media capabilities

Some marketing automation tools integrate with Facebook and Twitter, enabling you to control social advertising or build social apps from within the service. Some also offer social media monitoring, to pull comments made on social media platforms into your CRM. These features are usually nice-to-haves, but it might be worth considering carefully whether they would actually be useful to you.

Training and Set-Up

Ask how long it will take your company to implement the marketing automation software, and ask for the overall cost, as this information is not particularly well advertised by any software providers.

What is ClickFunnels?

My preferred platform for marketing, sales automation, and email marketing platform is ClickFunnels. ClickFunnels is a fairly mature service developed by Russell Brunson and his team. It's now been up and running for more than 3 years at the time of this review.

I learned about ClickFunnels through Russell's new book *DotCom Secrets: The Underground Playbook for Growing Your Company Online*. I highly recommend it to anyone wishing to learn how to sell products.

Unlike competitor products which allow you to create single standalone pages, ClickFunnels focus on **building different types of marketing funnels**.

A funnel is basically a series of pages your visitors go through to reach a certain goal. For example, a simple **Lead Capture Funnel** might consist of two pages which collect a visitor's email address and then sends them to a Thank You page when signing up. Alternately, you could have more sophisticated sales funnels, made up of multiple pages which sell to or engage with a visitor through each step of the funnel.

With ClickFunnels you can easily create:

Optin/Lead Capture Funnels

Used to capture email addresses of your visitors and grow your mailing list.

Sales Page Funnels

Used to sell products and services, with the ability to add any upsells/downsells to your sales process.

Webinar Funnels

Used to help people register for your webinars.

Membership Sites

Generates a recurring income by creating a full blown membership site.

Templates

ClickFunnels include a distinctive set of templates for each different funnel type that you create. Or you can start from scratch, building pages directly using the ClickFunnels editor.

Editor

The editor is where ClickFunnels really shines. This enables you to easily put together different pages in your funnel through an easy point and click interface. No coding is required and anyone can create something distinctive and professional. Everything is live, so you can see all your design changes in real-time.

ClickFunnels give you quite a bit of flexibility in creating your pages. For example, you can easily move elements around, placing them wherever you want, which is something the Leadpages editor does not allow.

Getting Started with ClickFunnels

I was immediately impressed by the ClickFunnels on-boarding

process. Their smart sales strategy includes offering you a free ClickFunnels t-shirt just for watching the introductory training videos. In approximately 10 minutes, the training videos give you a good overview of how ClickFunnels works.

Creating your first funnel is easy. Click the **Add Funnels** button and you are taken to a screen showing all the funnel types available. If you are unclear with what each funnel does, you can watch an embedded video which explains how it works.

Pick the Funnel you want and click the **Create Funnel** button. You will be asked to give your funnel a name. ClickFunnels will then generate a set of pages for you, based on the funnel you've chosen. So, for a sales funnel you would get:

Pages can be removed from the funnel by hovering and clicking the giant 'X' next to the page. For each page in your funnel, you can select from the available templates. Each template is professionally designed and there is a good selection to choose from. Plus, more are being added all the time.

The basic building block of a ClickFunnels page is a **section**. A typical funnel might have a header section, an above the fold content section and a footer section. A long form sales page might also have a section for highlighting specific features or a section for testimonials.

If you don't see a template that matches your current vision, I've found that it's just as easy to start from scratch. This can be done by picking any template and then quickly deleting each of the sections on the page.

ClickFunnels is flexible enough to support all types of designs. Sections are then further divided into **column rows**. You can have anywhere between one and six columns. Finally, you insert various ClickFunnels elements into the column. Basic widgets include Headline, Image, Text, Button, Input forms and Video elements although you can also include more advanced elements like:

- SMS Signup
- Survey
- Pricing Table
- Video Unlocker
- Facebook Comments
- FAQ Blocks
- Countdown Timers
- Custom HTML

Run your mouse over any section, row, or element, to highlight it and click slide in the contextual editor from the right-hand side where you can change its properties.

Background colors, margins, fonts, alignment can all be changed, as well as element specific properties like a specific image URL for the Image element. It's all quite intuitive once you've played around with it! Personally, I've been quite impressed by the editor as it strikes a nice balance between flexibility and ease of use.

If you are selling a product, then you want to integrate with a payment processor. ClickFunnels directly supports Backpack CRM, InfusionSoft, and Clickbank. Alternately, I recommend using the Stripe integration since it is free to sign up and use.

Tracking

In addition to helping you create each of the pages in your sales funnel, ClickFunnels also helps you track how each page in your funnel performs. At the top of each page, you can see in real-time the total number of visitors for each page in the funnel, how many visitors clicked on the next button of the page, and the conversion rate. You will also see a graph showing your stats over a specified time period.

Split testing is also baked into ClickFunnels which is essential for helping you **optimize the conversion rate** of your funnels. Click in the **Split Test** tab to see the stats of all your existing split tests as well as a button to create a **New Split Test**. Setting up new split tests is quite easy. The best way is to clone an existing page and then tweak it from there.

Actionetics and Backpack

When ClickFunnels was first released, it was all about creating…well, funnels. But Russell had even bigger ambitions for the product and that's how Actionetics and Backpack came about.

Actionetics

Actionetics is a replacement for your favorite email service provider. With Actionetics, you can see everyone who has opted into your lists through your ClickFunnels in the Contact Profiles page. Each of your leads receives an **Action Score**, based on the frequency of the contact, monetary value, and social scores. It basically gives you an idea of which leads are more likely to buy from you.

You can use Actionetics to send email broadcasts, and the email builder allows you to design nice looking emails. **Action Funnels** are Actionetics' way of creating autoresponders with some limited marketing automation features.

While some of its features are interesting, Actionetics still can't compete with a full-fledged email service provider like ActiveCampaign, Drip, or ConvertKit. Personally, I just prefer a standalone service where I'm not tied into an all-in-one solution.

Backpack CRM
One of the best ways to boost the sales of your product is to have a great affiliate program that attracts some top affiliates. If you offer a commission of 30% or higher, you can encourage people to sell your products with a high converting funnel, so they will spend their money to buy your products.

That's what Backpack can do for you. It's essentially a complete affiliate platform for ClickFunnels that you can attach to any of your created funnels. Inside Backpack, you can add everything you need for affiliates to promote your product including affiliate links, email swipe copy, and banner ads. You can also set up your affiliate payouts and see how well each of your affiliates is performing. There's even support for second tier commissions which is an extremely powerful incentive.

Pricing
There are two models I recommend for ClickFunnels when it comes to pricing.

ClickFunnels, Everwebinar, and Active Campaign

At $97 + $49 a month, this includes all the features of click funnels and the ability to have up to 100,000 subscribers in your list. The pros include all the features of ClickFunnels and the Power of Marketing Automation using Active Campaign, at a lower entry cost. The cons include hitting a break-even point with the Etison Suite at 10,000 subscribers in Active Campaign and that the cost increases with the more contacts you have in your list. Everwebinar is $497.00 year.

ClickFunnels, Etison Suite, and Everwebinar

At $297.00 a month, this includes everything, including Actionetics and Backpack. You also receive unlimited funnels, pages and visitors and you can have an unlimited number of contacts in your list. You can have Etison suite Free for 6 months when you buy Funnel Hacks. The pros include access to all the features of ClickFunnels and the Power of Marketing Automation using Active Campaign. You will never have to migrate to another marketing platform for your business and you can have up to 100,000 additional subscribers for no additional charge. The cons include the higher entry cost.

Marketing automation is the key to increased sales and increased freedom in your life and business. As I specialize in marketing automation in my business, I can help you channel this power into your business. Turn on the **Profit Faucet™** in your life and business, today! If you would like to try ClickFunnels and the Funnel Hacks Course, let me know, since I can direct you to a FREE Trial. You can also get Etison Suite of ClickFunnels for Free for 6 months by buying their Funnel Hacks Courses course.

Chapter 10 - Hiring a Business Coach

As you can see from the content we've covered in this book so far, running a business takes a wide range of skills plus there are numerous issues to monitor and handle. When you are distracted by the endless administrative requirements of running your own business, it can be challenging to concentrate on the central mission at hand. You may also struggle to set realistic financial milestones and marketing strategies, when you don't have the business experience to predict market changes. A business coach can help you view your business as a whole, and keep you on track so you meet your goals.

Coaching on a Budget

If you have a low budget for coaching, start by purchasing a few manuals and books on small business management. Read and then re-read these books as you establish your business, as you will only be able to apply some of the advice once you are confronted with various challenges. I find it's also helpful to read the book reviews on Amazon, as you can learn whether the book has helped others, and how they have used the guidance to build their own small business. Online courses, podcasts, and webinars are other low-cost options for business coaching.

While this self-taught coaching will potentially give you a good thorough overview of how to run a small business, the information will not be targeted specifically to your business. You can consolidate this by networking on professional sites such as LinkedIn, discussion boards or joining a local MeetUp for entrepreneurs. Networking gives you the opportunity to brainstorm issues or keep pace with market changes while talking with other entrepreneurs in your industry or local area.

Targeted Coaching

A business coach will help you work from the ground up, structuring your business and planning ahead so your marketing and financial management are effective at expanding your profitability. So, what qualities should you look for in a business coach?

A Clear Vision for the Role of Coach

Ask your coach to clearly explain their role and responsibilities as coach. This explanation should clearly demonstrate that they have a focused active plan for supporting your business. Be wary of anyone who makes enthusiastic generalized or unrealistic promises, such as "Within three months, you'll be Number One in the state!" You don't want empty promises – you want a clear practical strategy which includes measurable goals.

Proven Experience

Your business coach should have a successful entrepreneurial background, so they are familiar with all the challenges you will face when building your business. Remember, "proven experience" should include a few failures or setbacks along the way. In the words of Henry Ford: "Failure is only the opportunity to begin again, only this time more wisely." If a potential coach boasts of an unbroken track record of successful business ventures, you have to assume they are either concealing some details or they don't have much experience at all. You want a coach who has the wisdom of experience, who recognizes the potential for failure at first hand through personal experience, so they can guide you through the pitfalls, and also support you with a positive and practical attitude when things don't go exactly to plan.

A Strong Rapport

Your business is your passion and your future security, so you need to trust your business coach implicitly, while also feeling confident that they have faith in your skills and judgment. The relationship between entrepreneur and coach is a type of partnership, so you need to feel comfortable communicating with each other, particularly if you happen to disagree about a strategy or do not understand why your coach is recommending a particular technique. There is no point working with a coach who has no faith in your business idea, or who is more focused on their own personal agenda. Find a coach who will be a true mentor, helping you become independent and resourceful.

Your coach should also demonstrate intuitive reasoning about how you handle your business, giving you tailored advice based on their observation of your performance. They should be able to point out the strengths and weaknesses of your business leadership and explain this to you in a way that makes you feel inspired and motivated to improve.

Recommendations

A successful entrepreneur doesn't necessarily have the skills to be an influential and supportive business coach. Ask your network for recommendations, so you can work with someone whose entrepreneurial experience is matched by their proven reputation as a good coach.

Avoid any business coaches who try to drum up business through unrealistic spam. I saw an advertisement recently for a business coach who offered a "guaranteed" luxury lifestyle, complete with photographs of a sports car and a young woman sitting on a beach with her laptop. You want guidance to build up your business, you are not daydreaming about winning the lottery.

A Shared Vision for Success

You and your coach should be on the same page about what you are trying to achieve here. If you know what you want, but you're not sure how to articulate it, the coach should have the experience and insight to help you define success on your terms… and figure out the best way to achieve it!

Seven Questions

Here are seven questions to ask them about their business. The quality of their answers will tell you everything you need to know about whether you can trust them to help you with your business.

"Can you give me an embarrassing example of how your own coaching business is not currently living up to your core values? What are you doing to change that?"

Everybody has their weaknesses. And you'll never trust a coach with your weaknesses if they won't own up to some of theirs.

"Who is your ideal coaching client? What kind of person - not what

kind of business - do you love working with?"

If a coach doesn't know the type of person they can be passionate about serving, they haven't done the real work of branding and marketing. If they don't know why they feel passionate and driven, they will struggle to help you with your business.

"Have you ever owned or run a business that failed?"

Even if they've had success before, can you really know why? Find out how they dealt with failure - that's the window you need to see who they are professionally and personally.

"What systems do you have in place in **your business** to manage expenses and stabilize cash flow?"

A prominent industry figure recently stated that you don't need to know about business to be a business coach. This is straight crazy. A coach doesn't just have to know about business, they better know how to run one ... their own!

"What is your definition of success?"

Does the coach's definition match your own definition in the ways that matter? You want a coach who shares your perspective on what makes a meaningful and rich life - how else will they help you reach your goal?

"What is business coaching anyway? Sounds like some mish-mosh of consulting and therapy ... do I have that right?"

Your coach's ability to answer this question is critical to the long-term success of your relationship.

"We've been talking for 45 minutes now - what does your intuition tell you about the dysfunction in my business or in me as the leader?"

If they haven't gotten under your skin with at least one tough question yet, or worse haven't thought of one, they're probably in the wrong profession.

Behind these seven questions is the one big one you're really looking for an answer to: *Is this person for real?*

Setting Up a Coaching Contract

Once you have chosen a coach, you must set up a contract or agreement, outlining all the essential elements of your arrangement. This agreement supports both of you – protecting your time, money, and intellectual property. It also clearly defines what you both expect to achieve from the relationship. Any successful relationship is symbiotic, meaning you both give each other something of value, so you can both thrive. A coaching relationship is no different.

Throughout my career, I have relied on the support and wisdom of coaches and I have also coached clients to help them reach the next level and beyond for their business. Simply hiring a coach is a positive acknowledgement of your dedication to improvement and growth. Successful people are committed to continued learning, and hiring a coach is a great way to push yourself to improve upon the person you were yesterday. Like anything, when you want the best from your coaching relationship, you need to put in the groundwork and outline exactly what you both want to achieve. I love working with crazy passionate entrepreneurs and I choose my clients as much as they choose me – when I work with someone, I want to feel I am helping them make a difference.

Here are the five essential points I always want to cover in any coaching agreement in order to establish a productive symbiotic relationship. I hope you find these points helpful.

- Define the relationship ("DTR"). Just as you would define the parameters and goals of your relationship with your significant other, your DTR conversation with a potential coach should happen at the outset. Your coach should have a clear understanding of your wants and needs, and should be confident about your level of commitment.

  I start all my coaching relationships with a business diagnostic, to produce a 25 page report about your business, including strategies to improve it. Alternately, we can schedule a VIP day where we work together for 6 hours in person or over Skype to create the business diagnostic together and map out your business plan for the next 12 months. Besides creating a workable plan, this business diagnostic has the second purpose of testing how we work together. If we decide my coaching skills are not the right fit for your business, you can still take ownership of the business diagnostic and use this information when you work with a different coach. The business diagnostic can still help you make informed decisions about the future path for your business.

- The exchange: All valid contracts require some kind of exchange or "consideration" so your agreement should include a detailed description of the coaching services alongside a comprehensive payment plan.

- Rendering services: This section should explain how the coach will render their services, with options including in-person consultations, phone conferences, texts, and SnapChat (please use discretion with this last option). Each communication medium has its strengths and weaknesses so figure out what is best for you and work from there. Don't feel pressured to migrate to a medium that doesn't fit your communication style or skill set. Also take care not to compromise your confidentiality or intellectual property by sharing information on social mediums, such as SnapChat, which pose complex privacy risks.

- Termination: Every contract should include some agreed terms for termination. Personally, I like to establish that the relationship is recurring monthly, so we can amicably finish the coaching if the relationship is not productive or once we have achieved everything we have set out to accomplish. In this case, you would agree on a monthly fee for the consultation. Some of the reasons I have suggested terminating a coaching partnership include the client missing several meetings or if they are clearly disregarding my advice. On the rare occasions this has happened, the client has already decided the partnership does not fit their vision, so I like the option of a monthly renewal which gives us the chance to end the partnership openly and honestly when we mutually agree this is the best decision.

- Guarantee: You need to understand that your coach cannot guarantee any specific outcomes regarding your business. While you might want to see concrete results, be wary of the coach who guarantees your income will increase by 20% in the first quarter or that your customer base will expand by a certain amount. You should trust your coach to *show* you how to achieve the best outcomes, so you can create realistic and measurable goals.

These five points establish a strong foundation for any coaching agreement, and I recommend you ask to have them included in any coaching agreement offered by the coach you decide to hire. If you have any specific questions about hiring a business coach, please don't hesitate to contact our office for more information.

In Summary

Essentially, your business coach is the wiser, more experienced, more far-sighted version of you – with the same vision for success, the same drive to succeed, just with the background and hands-on experience to make it happen. You will know you have found the right coach when you feel that connection and shared vision. When you are confident about being yourself, being honest about your strengths and weaknesses, because your coach has utmost confidence in your ability to succeed; and your coach is ready to guide you through the process to success.

Appendix – Tools of Marketing

I have been researching and testing marketing resources for more than 12 years, so now I can share this list of the best marketing tools I have personally used and tested. I use all these tools in my business daily, so I know they work and I can personally recommend them as the best and most essential resources for your business.

Social Media Automation tools

Dux Soup –
This is an excellent tool for expanding your influence on LinkedIn. Dux-Soup will "view" over 7,500 LinkedIn profiles a week, as if you were viewing them manually. Your prospects become aware of your profile, so they are more likely to link with you.
http://dux-soup.com

ManageFlitter –
This tool helps you consolidate and monitor your Twitter followers, so you can schedule your tweets more effectively, manage multiple accounts and more.
http://manageflitter.com

Buffer –
Buffer is a social media scheduling tool, enabling you to share posts across all your social media profiles according to your own posting schedule. It also provides the analytics you need

to make the most effective schedule and appealing content for your target audience. http://buffer.com

Email Marketing

Active Campaign –
http://activecampaign.com

Click Funnels - 10,000 to 200,000 Subscribers with ETISON Suite - https://peakprofitglobal.com/clickfunnels

Marketing Automation

Click Funnels –
http://peakprofitmedial.com/clickfunnels

Web Design and Landing Pages

Peak Profit Global
http://peakprofitglobal.com

Domain Name Registration and Shared Hosting

Name Cheap - http://namecheap.com

Word Press Hosting

Wp Engine - Fastest WordPress Hosting in the World & Best Support - http://peakprofitglobal.com/wpengine

Manage DNS and Hacker Protection

Cloud Flare – All my sites are registered with Cloudflare for their DNS to stop denial of service attacks by hackers – http://cloudflare.com

Wordpress Themes
(Awesome alternatives to Wix or Weebly)

Thrive Themes - https://thrivethemes.com

Kleo - https://seventhqueen.com/themes/kleo/

Payment Providers

In my experience, you need to be able to process payments with three merchant accounts, so you have a backup in case you are shut down on one for being too successful.

Stripe - https://stripe.com

Chase Payment Tech - https://www.chasepaymentech.com

Pay Pal - https://www.paypal.com

Authorized.Net - You're Bank Merchant Services will offer Authorized.net as a payment gateway and you will get your money from credit card processing within 24 hours vs 2 days for most other merchant providers. Request Authorized.Net Payment gateway is through your bank.

Coinbase – I use coinbase with a plugin for WooCommerce on my wordpress sites to accept Bitcoin for my services – http://coinbase.com

Password Management Tools

Last Pass - Manage and Securely Share Passwords - https://www.lastpass.com

Call Tracking & phone numbers

800 Link - Automated Attendant and Business Numbers - http://800link.com

Line2 - Automated Attendant and Business Numbers with Text Messaging - http://line2.com

Call Tracking Metrics - https://www.calltrackingmetrics.com

Call Rail - https://www.callrail.com

Lead Generation

Peak Profit Global - Pay per Click and SEO - http://peakprofitglobal.com

RVM Leads on Demand - Ringless Voice Mail and Voice Broadcast - http://rvmleadsondemand.com

Hunter - B2B - https://hunter.io

Clear Bit - B2B - https://clearbit.com/

Local Leads - B2B -
http://leadexperiments.com/localcontacts/go/

Video Capture
Snag It –Capture Photos and Video you're your screen -
https://www.techsmith.com/techsmith-launches-
snagit-13-060716.html

Screen-O-Matic - Picture in Picture Screen Capture -
http://screen-o-matic.com

Audio Recording
Audacity – Record Audio
http://**audacity**.sourceforge.net/**download**/